The Fool's Journey through the Tarot

~ Swords ~

2nd Edition

by Noel Eastwood

Book 3 The Fool's Journey series

All rights reserved, copyright © 2018 and 2020 2nd Edition Noel Eastwood

Noel Eastwood asserts the moral right to be identified as the author of this work. By payment of the required fees, you have been granted the non-exclusive and non-transferable right to access and read the text of this ebook on screen or in print form. No part of the text may be reproduced, transmitted, downloaded, decompiled, reverse engineered, stored in or introduced into any information storage or retrieval system, in any form or by any means, electronic or mechanical, known or otherwise yet invented, without the express permission of Noel Eastwood.

This novel is a work of fiction set in the context of Tarot and other esoteric wisdom. Characterisation, incidents and locations portrayed are the work of the author's imagination. No affiliation is implied or intended with any organisation or recognisable body mentioned within.

Contact the author, Noel Eastwood:
Email: info@plutoscave.com
Web: http://www.plutoscave.com
Facebook - @PlutosCave
Cover illustration: JoAnn

Editor: Kristal

Deck: Original Rider-Waite deck (1910)

A special thank you to my editor, Kristal, and my precious band of beta readers. To JoAnn, thank you for your cover artwork and ongoing support.

Books in this series:

The Fool's Journey Through the Tarot:-

Major Arcana - published – also available as an audiobook

Pentacles – published – soon in audiobook

Swords – published – soon in audiobook

Cups – coming late 2020

Wands – coming early 2021

Other books by Noel Eastwood:

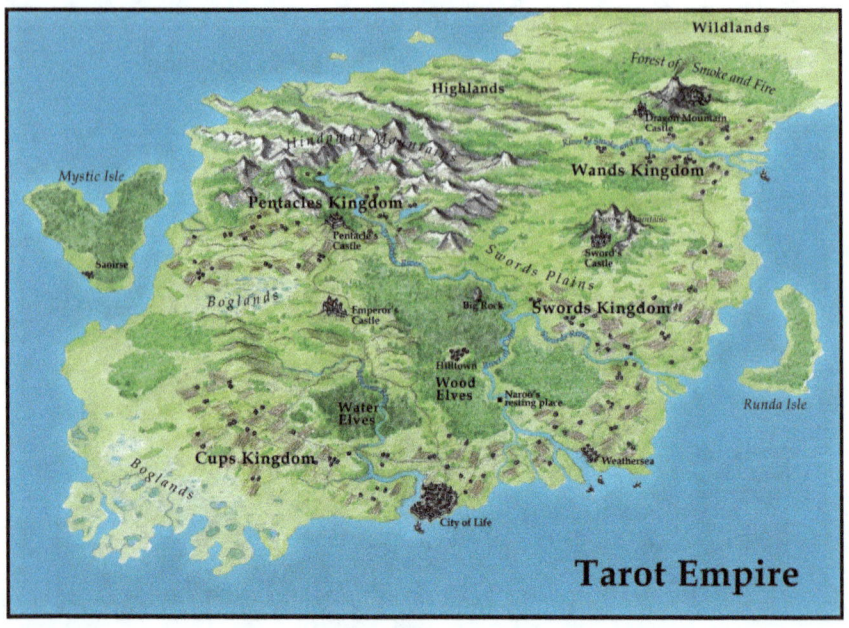

View the map online **at www.plutoscave.com**

Preface to the 2nd Edition

This is the expanded 2nd Edition of the third book in the Fool's Journey series.

Many Tarot readers consider the Swords suit as the most difficult to understand and interpret. In writing this book, I was mindful that the theme of the Swords suit is the Air element which corresponds with the western occult tradition of intellect and the conscious mind.

The Swords suit aptly illustrates the mental torment of being human. We often worry ourselves sick fearing what we don't understand. The conscious mind can also deny or invent irrational explanations to hide or disguise one's motives. The conflict depicted in the cards is the conflict of the mind: worry, stress, irrational explanations, magical thinking, lack of clarity and denial.

As with the first two books in this series, I have found the best way to illustrate each card's meaning is through the story of Follin, Eve and the friends they encounter on their journey through the Tarot Kingdoms. Follin's journey into the Swords Kingdom has provided ample opportunity to demonstrate the suit's conflicts as well as its positive attributes.

Originally written for Tarot practitioners the Fool's Journey Series has found a wider audience in those interested in personal growth. Through Follin we come to respect, and delight in, The Fool in all of us.

Please be mindful that the interpretations of the cards are mine alone. Each Tarotist has their personal eccentricities which will be apparent in their readings. This illustrates the power of melding imagery, symbolism with the vagaries of the human psyche - every reading is unique to the time, place, querent and reader. I would want it no other way.

Noel Eastwood
Canberra, Australia
October 2020
2nd Edition

Lao Tzu – Tao Te Ching

Become totally empty.

Quiet the restlessness of the mind,

Only then will you witness everything unfolding from emptiness.

Ace of Swords

Initiating an adventure of the mind.

On the morning they were to leave for the Swords Kingdom, the two Mystic Islanders, Follin and Eve, were introduced to their newly arrived escorts, the Swords Pages Natalie and Arthur. They were a young couple similar in age to Follin and Eve.

"We heard that you had Mystic Isle and Wildlander blood in you," said Natalie knowingly as she helped Eve carry her bags to the wagons. "I've been studying lineage, and it's such a fascinating subject. If we have time on our trip, which I'm sure we will, I'll teach you some of what I've learned," promised the young Swords Page.

Eve was still a little apprehensive around members of the court, and the Swords Page, Natalie, was quite different from Alice and her

Pentacles friends. Eve found her overly forward and excessively talkative. This was unlike Alice's conversations which were down to earth, leading towards doing something practical. Feeling a little out of her depth Eve kept her end of the conversation light and listened to the Swords Page politely.

"We are so lucky!" gushed Natalie, not noticing that Eve rarely said more than *'yes'* or *'that's interesting'*. "We'll have two apprentice mages with us, that will be so much fun. I bet you'll enjoy seeing our Swords Windmages, they can fly. Truly, they fly in the air! Our castle is built in a rocky valley, up against an enormous triple-peaked mountain. It's perfect for the wind currents to swirl our mages up to their sacred cave on the mountain top. How incredible is that?"

This news did make Eve start. "What? Fly? You mean they leap up and fly through the air?" she asked, a baffled look on her face.

"Oh yes, they have a wing that they hold on to. You know, a wing, like a bird's wing. The Windmage holds onto the wing and jumps off the top landing of our castle. The wind then lifts them up into the sky," replied Natalie, almost breathless with excitement.

"The Windmages can fly on the air currents for hours, it's so amazing." Natalie felt proud to be the one to explain something of such importance and wonder to the two newcomers. "It's glorious to watch them flying in circles as they gain height to get to the very top of the mountain."

"Do they ever fall?" gasped Eve, she couldn't help but ask the most obvious of questions.

Natalie was quiet for but a moment. "Actually, they do, sometimes."

"Oh, that is terrible, remind me not to take up any invitations to go flying with this wing-thing," declared Eve. The young Swords Page was trying so hard to impress her that Eve struggled not to laugh out loud.

"Oh, I wouldn't go up in the air with the wing either, it's way too dangerous." By now the two had stopped at the wagon where an assistant helped load Eve's bags. A moment later, Arthur led Follin over.

"We've had an enlightening talk about the games we play," announced Page Arthur. "Follin is just fascinated, he wants to start learning as soon as we have time tonight, after our evening meal, don't you, Follin?" he asked, a bright, friendly smile on his youthful face.

"I am sure that I will have nothing better to do than play cheekers with you tonight, Arthur," replied Follin politely, his jaw set tightly so as not to betray the frustration that had been building since meeting their Swords escorts.

"It's not 'cheekers', Follin, it's 'checkers'." Arthur chuckled lightly. He put his arm around Follin's shoulders like they were best friends. "Come on, I'll show you inside our wagon, that's where our games are stored. I might have enough time to show you some before we leave."

Follin caught Eve's eye and rolled his own. "I can't wait, Arthur," he said woodenly.

Natalie stared at Follin as though she had forgotten something important. Suddenly she grabbed one of the bags about to be passed into the back of the wagon and pulled out a sheaf of paper.

"Follin, I'm so sorry, I forgot to give you these. The Emperor asked me to present you with this picture-map for your next journey. It's to help you understand our Swords Kingdom." She finished with a broad, proud smile as she handed the pictures over.

The young Mystic Islander took the proffered papers. He quickly scanned the first few pictures then carefully put them into his pack.

"Thank you, Natalie, these will help me understand what I'm to learn in your Kingdom."

The journey to the Swords Kingdom had always been arduous and dangerous. The roadway initially skirted the farmlands to the south of the Pentacles castle. It then wound its way through a series of thickly forested hills to eventually cross the Pentacles River south and east of the Hindamar Mountains. From here the party would trek east across the Swords Plains to the Swords castle.

In the south of the Swords Kingdom were many farms while to the north stood a single mountain topped by three peaks, this was their destination. The Swords castle was built right into the mountain's towering cliff walls. It was here that the Swords Windmages flew their wings. The road that led to the castle itself passed along a rock-strewn valley, a perfect sanctuary to defend in times of danger.

From the moment they started their journey Sir Dale began teaching Follin the art of the sword. Although his sword was one of Master Pews, Follin clearly struggled in learning swordsmanship.

"Lad, we'll leave off for today," announced Sir Dale one afternoon after another frustrating lesson. "I think the Swords will be happy to teach you the art of the bow, which I believe you have an instinct for." Follin had brought down a large goose for dinner a few nights into their trek which provided them with an excellent meal. "I'll introduce you to the Swords archers, Follin. They'll be pleased to have someone of your calibre join them in training."

Arthur noticed Follin's discomfort after each lesson. An excellent swordsman himself, Arthur was keen to help his new friend and asked Sir Dale if he could help in some way. During their lessons together, Follin discovered that some of Arthur's moves were innovative and could be adapted to his own build and flexibility. Under Arthur's tutorship, Follin began to feel he may one day be able to defend himself with his sword.

"So you helped make this with Master Pew?" inquired Arthur as he carefully examined Follin's sword. "It's a cracking beauty!" he exclaimed as he swung it about, first in his right hand then in his left. "It's as light as a feather and as fast as a plains wolf. Master Pew's weapons are highly prized in the Kingdoms you know. This isn't one of his standard swords like he makes for the soldiers either, this one is rare indeed."

The young Page rubbed at his hairless chin as he held the blade up to the light and mused, "There's something inscribed on it too, I wonder what it says..."

Arthur stopped talking to swing Follin's sword back and forth once more. It whistled as he whipped it vigorously through the air. He laughed with delight as, spinning on his heels, he thrust at imaginary foes. Reluctantly he handed the sword back to Follin.

"Eve said that you went into the mountains to make it," he continued, half question half statement. Arthur was envious but also very curious.

'*These Swords people want to know everything about everything,*' thought Follin.

"Yes, I went into the Hindamar Mountains with Master Pew and his apprentice, Justin."

"What did you do when you were in the mountains, Follin? You don't need to tell me your smithy secrets, but please, tell me what you can. This is seriously interesting," pleaded Arthur.

Follin thought for a moment. "Well, I can tell you some things. We went into the mountains, to a special place that I had to intuit with my witching stick. That's how I found the iron ore, and it showed me where to build my kiln too. They call a kiln a 'dragon' when it's made in the mountains. It took a whole week just to forge the wolf, that's the raw iron. Then we took it down the mountain, poor donkey was loaded with so much ore we had to help him carry it. The scabbard was made by Master Lexis, the leathersmith."

"Wow, Master Lexis! He makes our scabbards and belts as well. He has a reputation for fine workmanship. He has a special leather-magic that he weaves into some of his belts and scabbards. Tell me, what is he like?" asked Arthur, now leaning with Follin against their wagon as they waited for the evening meal to be announced.

"I've only met him that one time, when he finished my scabbard." Follin was beginning to feel a little more comfortable telling stories to his attentive friend. "When I went to pick up my scabbard, Justin suggested we leave a jug of ale at his house on our way to his workshop. Master Lexis has a taste for a particular type of ale, and there's only one tavern in the Kingdom that brews it." Follin smiled to himself as he recalled the time when he and Justin had to visit half a dozen villages to find that particular ale. "It's a nicely matured ale too, we call it 'old'. It smells and tastes different to the 'new' beer at the other taverns. Anyway..." the two were now chatting like old friends.

Eve watched them and noticed how animated Follin was, she also saw that Arthur hung on every word. This was new, Follin was usually so quiet and shy, but Arthur made him feel valued and accepted. She knew how badly Follin struggled to communicate, but since they'd met the two

Swords Pages he was starting to show more confidence in speaking his thoughts.

"Boys!" she called as she walked across to them. "It's meal-time. The cooks have made lentil and mushroom pie and they smell delicious. Come on, hurry, before the soldiers eat them all." She laughed when she saw Follin caught between wanting his meal and wanting to stay and talk.

As usual, Follin's fae pup, Sox, was always at Follin or Eve's side. Whenever Follin went into the forest for his meditations, Sox was right beside him. At meal times he would only take food from his master or mistress' hand, but he did make an exception for Frailbones when he had a scrap of meat left over from his meal. Sox still needed frequent rest breaks with Eve and Frailbones on their wagon seat. Once he was rested he would leap down and race to play with Eve's elemental, Molly, or trot along beside Follin's horse at the front of the column.

At this stage there were only two Swords people in the wagon train, Pages Arthur and Natalie. The Pentacles had planned to meet with the Swords' cavalry squadron on the forest track but thus far there was no sign of them.

A few days into their journey, Sir Dale called Page Arthur to his side.

"Arthur, are you sure we were to meet your troops at this creek crossing? Is it possible it could have been another one? Did Sir William say anything about running late or any alternative meeting places?" asked Sir Dale, his face creased with concern.

Fortunately they had seen no sign of Wildlanders, it had been a quiet trip. On every other occasion the wagon trains were sure to encounter small bands of marauding Wildlanders resulting in frequent skirmishes along the forest roads. Generally, it was nothing too serious, a flight of arrows, a rush to grab a wagon load of grain or goods and it was over. Sometimes there were wounded but rarely were lives lost, but on this trip, it was just too quiet.

"Sir William must be held up somewhere. We've had reports of several wandering bands of Blue-beard Wildlanders. They come from the Wands' side of the Hindamar Mountains, in the lowlands. They like to paint themselves blue to appear frightening, which they don't, they just look silly," answered Arthur. "They're a lot more warlike than the Hindamar highlanders, the Brown-caps. So it's possible that Sir William is fighting the Blue-beards somewhere. Maybe he's been held up defending one of the farming villages on his way to meet us."

Sir Dale mused for a moment before ordering his wagons to resume their journey.

"Stay by my side this morning, Arthur. I'm not happy travelling this deep into the forest without the Swords escort," called Sir Dale over his shoulder as he urged his horse to the front of the train.

It was during their evening meal that a lone Swords soldier arrived. He was escorted to Sir Dale by one of Sergeant Lards' forward scouts.

"Greetings, Corporal Pope, I've been expecting your troops for some days. We were worried that something had happened to you," called Sir Dale as he stood to greet the exhausted Swords Bowman.

"Greetings, Sir Dale. Sir William sends his apologies," said the powerfully built young man. "We were supposed to meet you at yon creek but we've been held up guarding one of the villages. Our patrol is at Midlow Village, a day's ride from here. The Wildlanders have burned a few barns and taken some of the farmers' cattle and sheep. Sir William is with his cavalry trying to get the beasts back. The poor villagers are fed up with these raids. It seems that the Wildlanders are after everything they can get their hands on before winter sets in. Our men have tried to be everywhere at once but the Wildlanders still get through and create havoc."

"Is it the Blue-beards again? Have you seen any of the other Wildlander clans recently?" asked Sir Dale. He invited the Bowman to sit with him at his campfire and brought out one of the kegs of ale from his private wagon. He poured a mug for himself and the fatigued Swords Bowman.

"Most certainly, sir. Those scoundrel Blue-beards, sir, they're the most common ones hereabouts. The Wands see a lot of them too," replied the soldier emptying his mug in two thirsty mouthfuls.

"We're mostly troubled by the Brown-caps. I find myself admiring their courage in braving the perils of the high mountain passes to avoid our Mountaineer commando patrols," offered Sir Dale. "Our Pentacles Kingdom is blessed in many ways. We've got our Swords brethren on our eastern borders and the Wands covering the approaches through the foothills to the mountains in the north and east. Behind us are the rugged Hindamar Mountains which is a mighty barrier to all but the bravest of the Brown-cap Wildlanders."

"We've seen a few Brown-caps mixed in with the Blue-beards this time. There's not many, but they seem to get wilder when they join up together. It's like they try to outdo each other," added the corporal.

The two were soon joined by Sergeant Lards and Captain Bleecher to discuss their situation. The chill in the air forced them closer to the fire for warmth as they chatted and enjoyed their evening meal, with a generous mug or two of the knight's ale.

Each evening the four youngsters huddled together around their own campfire beside their wagon. Holding a carved wooden horse, Arthur demonstrated its moves on his chess board.

"This is the Black Knight, Follin. He jumps like this, two to the side and one forward, but he can also go backwards and sideways. It's like an 'L' shape," he explained for the umpteenth time.

"Yes, I said 'yes' before. I get it," replied a frustrated Follin. He struggled to comprehend the complex rules of chess.

Eve was watching Follin cope as best he could with something he always struggled with, and that was to understand complex verbal instructions. She was sitting with Natalie chatting about the social set at the Pentacles royal court. They often joked and giggled at how staid and boring the Pentacles could be. From the corner of her eye she watched as Follin tried to pay attention - but he just couldn't get it.

"Arthur, why not play a game of checkers instead? He's much better at that game," she offered, trying her hardest to help her husband.

"You think so?" Arthur looked at Follin and finally recognised the sour look on Follin's face. "Oh, yes, sure. I'll pack the chess away for some other time. Is that OK with you, Follin?" asked Arthur, trying to please his guest.

"Yes, and I hope you are ready to be beaten to within an inch of your Swordly life," challenged Follin, his face now showing some signs of interest.

That night Eve dreamed that she was with Molly and the High Priestess in the forest.

"Tonight, Eve, you will be taught by your elemental. She will take you into her world of the senses and teach you how to feel, smell and sense from her perspective." Hera paused to allow this to sink in. "I want you to meld with Molly, become a mole and expand your senses to embrace hers. Do not be afraid, go with the flow, trust Molly."

Eve could feel Hera's energy and almost swooned from the force of it. She made an effort to relax even deeper than usual so that she might more easily meld with her elemental.

It felt warm, she could feel the elemental mole's fur and smell the rich, diverse scents of the soil and its organic matter. It was strange not to see, but it was much like getting out of bed in the dark. Eve settled and went with the flow of her experience.

She rode waves of happiness feeling the earth's energy as rays of warmth. Eve felt her body open up to allow this force to penetrate every cell in her being. She felt the soil bursting with life and forces she had never known before. With a flash of understanding, Eve knew why certain plants needed certain soils; why some trees grew beside a stream or on a hill, or preferred wet or dry soils. So much information flowed into her: the healing powers of each plant, each tree, each vegetable and even which clays to use as healing poultices. It was sensory heaven. Eve was no longer 'Eve', she was simply a part, a fraction of her environment.

Then something shifted and she began to feel uncomfortable, she wanted to escape but couldn't. Eve felt trapped, afraid to even move fearing discovery. What if an owl saw her, or a fox or wolf? What if a snake crawled into her burrow? Eve was now Molly, a blind mole, one single entity of the many beings reliant on the living soil surrounding her.

"Eve, this is not your last lesson of this kind, it is your first. Let go and you will breeze through your lessons. Learn to cope with feelings, do not fight them," said Hera as the young woman drifted off into a deep sleep.

Follin's Meditation – Ace of Swords

Each night Follin meditated on one of the pictures provided for this stage of his journey through the Tarot Empire. The first picture was of a hand clutching a sword which pierced a crown. An olive and a palm branch draped over the crown's edge. He interpreted this as peace and success against worry and loss. Rising above the sword pommel were six flames which suggested imagination and inspiration.

'This probably means that a king must have a clever mind to claim this crown,' Follin thought.

He closed his eyes to enter the picture and noticed the hills. Turning his gaze to view the other elements in the picture he felt a brilliant radiance enter his being. His mind became crystal clear and he saw the entirety of the Swords Kingdom from above. For the first time Follin felt excited, impatient to get on with his Swords journey. He dearly wanted to keep that sense of clarity which he'd so rarely experienced before.

Instinctively Follin reached out and grasped the sword with his hand, it felt like it belonged there. It was very much like his own sword, crafted by Master Pew. It suddenly dawned on him that a king must seek clarity in all things. With this sword Follin sensed that he could cut through excessive emotion, unsound logic and delusional fantasy.

From his earlier studies with the Major Arcana archetypes he already knew that neither wild passions nor rigid rationalisations formed truth. Truth was found in the middle ground and a wise ruler needed to understand this before he made a decision.

Two of Swords

Anticipation; closed emotions; stopping internal dialogue; intellectual change point; seeking clarity through silence; separating logic from feelings; waiting patiently to act decisively.

Eve spent most of her travel time sitting at the front of the wagon with Frailbones, their aged Pentacles wagoneer. When Follin's fae pup, Sox, wasn't loping along beside his horse, he sat with Eve in the front of the wagon with Frailbones. The old man doted on Sox, he saved tit-bits from his meals for Eve to feed the growing pup. Eve noticed, however, that the closer they came to the Swords Kingdom the more morose Frailbones appeared. It hurt to see her friend becoming listless and depressed, so she decided to speak to Sir Dale.

"Lass, it happens every time we approach the River of Cups. We all sense his sadness and grief, it affects us all. His is a sadness that descends upon him that no-one can pierce." The Pentacles Knight paused to adjust the strap on his helmet. "There is a tale that Frailbones attempted to rescue an elf-princess from the Wildlander mages. It is said that he has never been the same since. We know it as the 'story never-told'. But Frailbones himself has never spoken of what happened at the River of Cups nor of the elf-princess. We only know of it from the whispered snippets from the elves who live in that region. Aye, 'tis a sad story indeed that makes a man grieve his entire life for a loss that happened when he was but a lad."

Eve nodded silently, bid her thanks to the Knight and went off to be by herself. She loved that old man, he had been the one person she could trust to be honest with her. Frailbones reminded her to be polite when she was rude, and he praised her when she made good choices. Eve realised that her old friend was mortal and within his staunch chest there lay a secret and a grief that even she could not touch nor heal.

The following day Natalie commented on how Arthur was spending more time with the Pentacles soldiers, more so than he had spent before. She said that Arthur was trying to understand the Pentacles soldier's funny ways. To a curious Swords any deviation from the norm made them want to know more.

"Follin, what is it with that Pentacles drummer? He plays but then he stops, then he gets the troops to sing, and then he gets them to skip and change foot, it's really weird," said the confused Swords Page.

"It's just their way, Arthur. The Pentacles are masters of every craft, and dancing, marching and singing come easily to them. Why don't you just relax and enjoy their funny ways. It took me a while to get used to them too, but now I really enjoy their marching. That drummer must be a hundred years old, but, wow, can he play." Follin turned his horse around and trotted back to the drummer now sitting in the lead wagon.

"Excuse me, Drum-Sergeant, this Swords Page wants to learn how to sing like a Pentacles man-at-arms," he called, smiling broadly at an embarrassed Arthur.

The Drum-Sergeant looked at the two young men for a moment. Catching Arthur's curious gaze he produced a long, melodious whistle from between his lips. He turned, and with a smile reached behind to bring out his drum and sticks. When he had settled back into his seat he began to tap to the rhythm of the soldiers marching in front of them. Then, with a loud drum roll, he introduced one of their many marching songs. His whistles informed the men which song was coming next, and the drum roll led them into it.

The men-at-arms sang along as the Drum-Sergeant led the song with a trip, a lick and then a drum roll. At the end of each song he would perform one of his many drum solos before initiating the next tune with its whistled introduction. His drum sticks would then click, roll or tap to signal for the soldiers to start singing.

But that wasn't the end of the fun. The Drum-Sergeant liked to play tricks on his men. Sometimes he would change the tempo, forcing the beat faster, then slowing it down. The men would accordingly speed up or slow down, even the cavalry horses knew the game and kept pace as well. Once in a while he would introduce a quick-step making the men skip and change their lead foot to the other. It made for fascinating entertainment both for those watching and for the bored troops.

After a while, Arthur, fascinated by the antics of the drummer and the troops, tried to match their pace and rhythm and even went so far as to sing along once he caught on to the words.

As they approached Midlow Village they met with a tired Swords forest patrol. Follin counted thirty archers and men-at-arms dressed in drab forest colours.

The men were chatty and bright-eyed, he liked them immediately. They were quite unlike the dour, well drilled Pentacles soldiers. At first glance they appeared to be unkempt, reckless and lacked discipline, but the truth was quite different. When ordered to patrol forward into the forest they instinctively split into groups, silently blending into the forest shadows as if the command was given telepathically.

The Swords Sergeant-at-arms, Sergeant Mills, stayed behind with the wagons and chatted with Sir Dale.

"This is grand news! I see you've added a few extra wagons to fill our empty pantries, Sir Dale. We've been waiting on them for some weeks now. Those Wildlanders are back in force, ambushing our patrols and interrupting our supply lines. They're trying to steal as much food as possible before winter. We're mighty glad to see you've made it this far without a single skirmish too," said the sergeant.

Sir Dale called for Follin and Arthur to join them. The small group rode to the front of the wagons to meet with Captain Bleecher.

"We've had our scouts patrolling every inch of our journey but we've not had any contacts with the Wildlanders, not yet anyway," said Sir Dale, rubbing irritably at his chin strap. He thought to remove his helmet but paused to listen to the Swords sergeant continue with his report.

"Aye, you've been lucky. They've played merry hell raiding our farms and villages. We've had very few up-front battles, mostly a few arrows, an ambush to grab what they can and then they're gone. The Wildlanders seem to have increased their attacks on the Wands Kingdom these past months too. Reports say they've had a series of pitched battles in the foothills of the Hindamar Mountains up north. We've sent several corps of our Bowman to help them. Those cunning Wildlanders don't normally stand up to a fight like they have in the Wands Kingdom recently. I've heard the Wands have even called on your Pentacles Mountaineers, and you know how fierce the rivalry is between them and their own Fearless commandos," smiled the sergeant.

Follin stopped scanning the tree line to look at the Pentacles Knight at mention of the Mountaineers and Fearless commandos.

"Our Mountaineers are specialist mountain fighters, Follin," answered the knight, "but we leave it to the Swords and Wands to do the heavy fighting elsewhere. If they have need of our Mountaineers we will gladly send them, we're in this together."

"I hardly know anything about your Mountaineers. Are they special soldiers?" Follin asked.

Sir Dale nodded. "Yes lad, they are specially trained to scout, patrol and fight at high altitude, up in the snow and ice. They spend a full year up in the high passes, much higher than where you and Master Pew went for your iron ores. They learn to survive in the snow and to climb impassable cliffs and glaciers. It's dangerous and we lose some of them each year. I spent some time with them in the Hindamar Mountains last autumn. They're a tough but cheery lot."

Captain Bleecher turned to Follin. "They're specialists in the highest sense of the word, lad. The Pentacles Mountaineers are always there, up in the mountain passes protecting the Empire. That's why so few Wildlanders make it through to raid our gardens and farms. They only accept volunteers too. They are the best of the best and every family dreams of having one of their sons in the Mountaineer Commando. Even the Wands' Fearless Commando respect our Mountaineers."

Sir Dale laughed. "Those Wands, my goodness, how they live to fight. While us Pentacles, we much prefer eating and singing..."

"...and us Swords prefer reading a good book and arguing with the tavern keeper, anything but fighting," added the Swords sergeant with a chuckle of his own.

Follin's mind took this all in. He was still trying to piece together each Tarot Kingdom's particular personality traits. These peculiar elemental characteristics fascinated him.

"Sergeant Mills, what commando do the Swords have? If the Pentacles have the Mountaineers and the Wands have the Fearless, what do you have?" asked a curious Follin.

The sergeant thought for a moment. "Well, lad, our elite archers are called Bowmen, they are the best archers in all of the Kingdoms. Our boys can shoot the eye out of a sparrow at a hundred paces. I've seen it done. All our archers loose one hundred arrows each morning before breakfast. That way they keep their accuracy and it makes their pulling-arm strong. Those bows take enormous strength to draw, far more than that toy you rely on." He pointed to Follin's Pentacles bow in his saddle bag. "That, my lad, is what our children play with. If you would like, I can give you a proper Swords bow and a quiver of arrows, you'll learn the real art of archery then."

Turning to look at his bow, Follin's eyes brightened. He had already used Arthur's Swords bow and it really did take enormous effort to draw.

"So, a hundred arrows before breakfast?" Follin asked, enthused by what he had just heard.

"That's right, lad, for each arrow that misses the target they have to loose another ten. That's what you'll see the lads doing every morn now that we've joined you," replied the Swords sergeant.

"OK, I'll take you up on that, Sergeant Mills. I'll join your archers every morning and learn the art of archery." Follin announced, much to the satisfaction of the sergeant. "But I'll still practice with my sword. Between what I learn from Sir Dale and Arthur, I'm hopeful that one day I'll be competent with both the sword and the bow."

"From what I've heard, lad, you can already shoot straight and true. Given a proper bow and a set of well fletched arrows, you'll soon be ready to join our Bowmen," assured Sergeant Mills.

Now that the Swords soldiers had joined the wagon train they quickly set about engaging in their own quirky behaviours. Arthur had forgotten to tell Follin that every Swords soldier belonged to a 'games clan'. Some enjoyed dominoes, some chess, others checkers and cards. They even had clans for word games and debating. But what fascinated Follin the most was how they enthusiastically competed against each other, clan versus clan.

Follin watched as one clan set up a large table for the popular 'Battles' game. The game of Battles was composed of small carved animals and men-at-arms soldiers, cavalry and archery figurines. At the end of each day's trek the Battle clans would quickly make ready their camp and then painstakingly set up their games tabletop. There they would place highly detailed miniature castles, rivers, hills and forests. Depending on whose turn it was to administer the game, two clans would then pull out their figurines and set about placing them in offensive and defensive positions. By the roll of a dice, and the master of ceremonies' book of rules, the game would commence, often not finishing until well into the night.

Follin was fascinated by the passion these Swords held for their *'games that strengthen the mind'* as the Swords Knight, Sir William, would call it. He rarely had time to join in, but he certainly enjoyed the rivalry and friendly banter of the clans, no matter which game they played. It certainly made the journey more pleasant and interesting, for everyone.

That evening Sergeant Mills took Follin to speak with Corporal Pope. They found him chatting with his Bowman troops, discussing forest-fighting tactics and how they might apply it at their next Battles competition.

"Corporal, young lad here wishes to learn the skills of archery from you Bowmen. I thought you might want to take him under your wing." Sergeant Mills gently pushed Follin towards the group huddled around their fire, now quietly observing this Mystic Islander whom they had heard so much about.

"It would be my pleasure, Sergeant, however, this young man here is quite the archer already. I heard he shot down a goose in flight the other day." Turning to Follin Corporal Pope said, "If it be the tools of a Bowman ye needs, lad, then ye can have one of the spare archery kits we have in the wagon."

"Wonderful. Thank you, lads," said Sergeant Mills in satisfaction. "I expect he'll be matching you lot at the archery range before too long." He chuckled lightly as he walked back to Sir Dale's fire.

"Don't worry, young Follin, we know you can shoot. It's the arm fatigue what gets those what don't practice every day," called one of the archers.

"Aye, lad, you're in luck, we're considered the best of the forester Bowmen. We're from this part of the Swords Kingdom you see. We know the forests and the people hereabouts. They be our villages what we'll come across on our trip to yon Swords Plains. We'll teach you to walk and hide, to sneak and shoot through the trees of the forests. I think you'll enjoy training with us, lad," said another.

"Why don't you go and fetch young Arthur? That lad's gone soft, he could do with some archery training too," added one of the older archers pointing towards the Page's wagon.

Follin nodded and excitedly raced across to his campfire. He grabbed Arthur by the arm. "Arthur, come on, we're going to train with the archer elites, the Bowmen!" At last, he had an excuse to escape Arthur's boring lectures.

They settled in for the night, pulling their wagons into a circular laager. Each wagon was positioned to cover the one beside it. Sir Dale paced about nervously, checking their defences. The Swords knight, Sir William, still hadn't arrived. Sir Dale noted that the soldiers, too, fidgeted with their weapons and mumbled among themselves around their fires.

"Captain Bleecher," whispered Sergeant Lards, the hand on the hilt of his sword twitched as he waved to his platoon of men-at-arms to prepare for action. "Sir, there are noises, horses, out in the forest track, sounds like they're coming from the direction of Midlow village."

"Tell Page Arthur to take Sergeant Mills and a squad of his archers and men-at-arms to cover the approaches to our camp. It may be a band of Wildlanders preparing for an assault on our wagons," whispered Sir Dale.

Follin, as Sir Dale's squire for the patrol, had begun running towards the knight the moment he saw Sergeant Lards urgently calling his men together. Follin stood beside the knight with his bow in his left hand, his other rested on his sword hilt.

"Sir, I can go and talk to the spirits of the forest if you want me to?" he offered. But Sir Dale was preoccupied and appeared not to have heard him.

"Captain, have the company and civilians prepare for an attack. Light some fires on the forest edges, it will give us light to see the enemy. Follin, if we're attacked, I want you to stand by me as my messenger." Sir Dale turned and looked at Follin to make sure he was paying attention. "I want you to watch my every move and be ready to run a message if I call you." Follin nodded, he was nervous and his head felt strange, like it was filled with light, fluffy clouds.

Sergeant Lards was busy ordering his men into position when they suddenly heard screams and yells coming from the track where Sergeant Mills and his men were sent to patrol. The people within the wagon laager waited nervously.

After some minutes of silence a lone Swords soldier jogged into the laager, his head bowed with exhaustion. Walking as quickly as his sore feet would allow, he gave his report.

"Sir, it was a Wildlander patrol. They've dispersed for now but we can't be certain they won't return," he panted.

"Hold your positions!" called Captain Bleecher to his troops. "Swords patrol have intercepted a bunch of Wildlanders. Sergeant Mill's lads have scattered them into the forest. Remain on alert and be prepared for incoming arrows."

Sir Dale turned to Follin. "Lad, it's time for you to enter the forest and do your earth magic like you did before. Don't forget the password when coming back or someone might mistake you for a Wildlander and pin you to a tree. Find out what the forest has to say."

Throughout their nervous wait, Eve had stayed beside Frailbones and Page Natalie. The three watched as Follin walked to the gap between the wagons facing the forest. He quickly placed his bow and arrows on the ground beside him and tightened his sword belt. Sox sat upright beside Eve, watching his master. The fae pup's ears pricked up as he sensed that an adventure was near at hand. He looked into the forest, back to his master, and then to Frailbones and Eve.

"Lass, 'tis just a skirmish, no need to get frightened and such," chatted Frailbones quietly, his eyes never leaving the forest edge, nor his hands from his bow. "Our Swords friends are fine warriors, they have an eye for night fighting and they've just seen the Wildlanders off. These Swords archers are Bowmen, the best of the best. But just in case 'tis a ruse and the Wildlanders have another patrol coming up through the forest, we'll stay alert."

Eve could feel her fingers clenched tightly around Frailbone's arm and had to force herself to let go. She transferred her grip to hold tightly onto Sox, drawing him close to her. He rubbed his nose into her neck and licked her face. That calmed her a little and helped her relax.

"Frailbones, I'm afraid. I can't see Follin anywhere now. Has he gone into the forest already?" she asked, fear perched on the edge of her voice.

"Young lad has gone into the woods, as ordered by his commander. No doubt he's doing his magicking like he did before at last fight." He glanced at his young ward. "He'll be fine lass, he has his magic."

Without warning, Sox shrugged free of Eve's grip and bounded into the forest straight to the bushes where Follin had disappeared.

"See, lass, Follin now has fae pup to look after him too. They will be fine. Fae dogs can see in the dark they say, if there be enemy the pup will warn his master."

At that moment, in her mind's eye, Eve saw the Hierophant and she instantly knew what to do to assist her lover.

'Molly, of course, I'll ask Molly to help him.'

Eve brought her mind to engage the earth-elemental who had adopted her during her Pentacle sojourn. She asked the blind elemental mole, Molly, to help Follin. There immediately came a warm response from her elemental and a relieved Eve came back to consciousness.

"Frailbones, I'm OK now. Follin has Sox and he now has my elemental. He'll be safe," she said and noticed that her shaking had stopped.

Follin crouched low as he entered the thick undergrowth on the forest edge. There came a sudden rustling noise from behind, it startled him. Before his mind could decipher the sound, Sox was beside him. The pup pushed up against Follin's leg and peered into the dim forest as though he knew to take up sentry duty for his master.

"Sox, you frightened me! I really didn't want you here, it's dangerous, you're just a pup," he whispered, half in fear and half in gratitude at his pup's presence. "Oh well, since you're here, keep a watch for me while I do my work."

Follin leaned his back against a large tree trunk and waited for his mind to settle before closing his eyes to send his awareness into the forest depths. Once again he felt the Pentacles change point, the balance between what is and what might be. As he slowed his breathing further, the essence of the forest embraced him. Within a few heartbeats he was almost overwhelmed by a flood of sensory impressions.

'I bet that's Molly,' he thought.

"Yes, it is me, I am here," came the blind mole's calming response.

Follin had to drop deeper into his meditative state as a new wave of raw forest smells, tastes, feelings and sounds enveloped him. He kept his focus on Molly until he could feel the warmth of her furry body. Her presence triggered strange sensory insights into the deep forest communities that surrounded him.

'Molly, can you please help me find out what the Wildlanders are doing?' he asked as he wondered how he might use Molly's broad range of sensory impressions. It was difficult not having visual images to rely on. Follin knew that Molly was a mole, blind to sight, and all of her impressions were formed from the other four senses.

'I know that you are struggling to decode my messages, so I will ask the trees to help me,' came Molly's quick reply.

As soon as he heard her response, Follin could sense the trees communicating with Molly. It was strange, Follin had his own means of decoding the tree's communications, but now he had the benefit of Molly's depth of experience and her unique interpretations.

The trees described how the Wildlanders had run away. But now there were others, safe others, travelling through the forest towards them.

Follin felt the warmth of friendship and communion between the trees and these new visitors. Although Follin had communicated with the forest countless times in the past, having Molly's help was like travelling up a steep hill holding onto the back of donkey's harness for support, it was effortless.

'It must be the Swords patrol returning,' he thought. Then another thought came to him. *'My goodness, those Swords Bowman are as silent*

as our Mystic Isle forest elves.' That frightening thought woke him from his trance.

Crawling softly on hands and knees he approached the wagon laager along the same path he took to enter the forest. He put his arm around Sox's neck then softly called the password to the soldiers who had been waiting for his return. They beckoned Follin to come into the firelight so they could identify him. Even though he was gone but a few minutes, the Pentacles soldiers nonetheless rigidly followed their orders.

"Righto, boys, it's the Isle lad and his pup, let them pass," called an old warrior, the knuckles on his sword hand crisscrossed with scars from past battles.

Another soldier spoke softly. "The lad's been magicking with the trees. What did ye learn, lad?"

"The Wildlanders have left, but someone else is out there," Follin replied as he began to make his way to find Sir Dale.

The soldiers nodded and smiled to each other, they felt a lot safer with Follin around than they let on.

"Aye, 'tis good to have a magicker with us, the lad's good at talking to the trees 'n spirits. We'll be missing the lad when we return home to our Kingdom," said one, watching the young Mystic Islander make his way to Sir Dale's wagon.

On hearing Follin's report, the Pentacles Knight drew his sword and called his reserves to order, he then marched them towards the forest path. Some of the soldiers held a burning torch. Follin and Sox joined them as the patrol strode carefully forward to make contact with this new Swords patrol.

Within the hour the two troops met. Sir Dale's patrol heard them just before they came into the light of their hand-held torches. The dull beat of the horses' hooves trampling the hard forest path, and the muffled jingle of their metal equipment, announced the Swords patrol arriving in the darkness. Leading them was an impressive, dark-haired cavalryman, it was Sir William, the Swords Knight.

"Hail and well met, cousin! I didn't think I'd ever get here," declared Sir William, his voice light and airy.

"Hail cousin, Will, it's good to see you've made it at last." Sir Dale stopped to examine the Swords cavalry by the light of the soldier's flaming torches. "I hear you've been busy with the Wildlanders again."

"Aye, the villains ambushed us on the track. We lost one of our cavalry, but we held our own. They escaped through the forest as they are wont to do. We've not had a stand up stoush for some months." Sir William blinked in fatigue. He slowly bent over and eased himself from the horse's saddle and placed his feet on the ground.

Sir Dale put his arm around his cousin's shoulders. "Will, I'll keep watch here for the night. Why don't you get your boys into camp, grab some food and some sleep, you look like you need it."

With grim pleasure the tired and hungry Swords cavalry and men-at-arms made their way to the Pentacles laager where Captain Bleecher met them. He waved them through nodding to those he recognised from previous patrols. He spoke soft words of encouragement noticing their wounds and the horse with its empty saddle.

'They've had a tough time of it indeed,' he thought.

At sight of the patrol the remaining Swords soldiers stationed at the wagons, broke into a light cheer as they called their comrades to share their campfires. The camp cooks hurriedly prepared a late supper, setting it on a series of trestles with jugs of ale and water.

"Aye, 'tis always a pleasure to visit with the Pentacles, they've the best damn cooks in the Empire," called one of the cavalrymen loudly - to the great pleasure of the cooks and their hard-working kitchen hands.

"Hey, lads! How about a game of Battles? We've enough clans to play a quick round," called one of the Bowman who had stayed behind to protect the camp. His suggestion was met with cat-calls, jeers and laughter. The last thing anyone wanted so late in the evening, and especially for those who had been out on patrol, was to play games.

Follin's Meditation - Two of Swords

In this, his second Swords meditation, Follin saw a woman, seated and blindfolded. She held a sword in each hand diagonally across her breast. In the background were several islands amid a gentle sea. The first thing that struck him was the lady's intense pose. He intuited that she was waiting, listening, probing, sensing the exact right moment to move, to swing her swords in the decisive act.

Follin sensed that the woman was calm, she was controlled and she had placed her irrational, emotive mind behind her. This gave her the clarity to focus on whatever it was that confronted her.

'This woman is in a state of perfect mental balance, her mind is clear and she has no fear, or desire. She appears prepared for action.'

As Follin pondered this thought, he realised that the woman was speaking to him.

"Follin, you have missed the most important point."

"What point is that, madam?" he asked.

"Do you remember the Two of Pentacles?" she asked him.

"Yes, I do. His intention was the 'change point', the point at which 'what could be' becomes 'what shall be'. He could harness the power of the Pentacles Ace to change things, like energy forms." Follin scratched his head. "Why?"

"I am of the Swords suit, what is my primary trait?" she continued.

"It is Air, intellect and conscious intent."

"Yes, but what does a sword do? Think in terms of metaphor… don't worry, I'll help you - a sword cuts. It can cut through denial, irrational arguments and excessive emotions. But my question is… to gain what?"

"I'm not sure what you mean." Follin was confused because he thought that she was the epitome of a clear mind, balance and freedom of emotion, but apparently not.

"Follin, let me make this easier for you. Come, meld with me," she commanded.

Follin felt himself become one with the blindfolded woman and immediately he understood her meaning.

"Oh, now I know! You harness the mental power of the Swords Ace to 'intend' the change point. You can use your clear mind to locate key words and phrases in someone's speech or writing which forecasts their intent."

"Yes, but I can't do that if my mind is wandering or if I'm feeling sad, fearful or lonely, can I?" *It was more statement than question, but Follin understood her point.*

"So you can identify someone's intention by their words? Wow, I wish I could do that. My mind goes all over the place when I listen to people. If I try to listen too hard it just makes me dizzy. I just get more confused," *he confessed.*

"That is my lesson: focus, attend, listen. Contemplate upon these words because this is how the Swords negotiators operate, they attend to words, body language, posture, tone of voice – every aspect of communication. They harness the power of Air, intellect, to find the change point in a debate or conversation. They listen to a debate, treaty or trade negotiation this way. By attending to the speaker's communication style our negotiators find the clues which show where the speaker is leading them. The master negotiator can then use that person's own words and manner to change the direction to where he wants it to go. Swords are the masters of negotiation because they have learned how to affect the communication change point. The key to understanding my lesson is to stop the mind. That means that you train your mind to cease all internal dialogue."

Follin thought for a moment. "Yes, I understand, I did a lot of training to achieve internal silence with the Major Arcana archetypes. This must mean that being focused, clear of mind and emotionally balanced, I can harness the power of the Air element? And to do that properly I need to stop my internal noise, my self-talk. Hmm, if I find the change point of my own mind, can I affect someone else's intention?"

"Yes, with a great deal of practice you most certainly can."

There was a nagging question he needed to ask the lady before she left him.

"Do you mind if I ask what those islands are for, the ones in the background, behind you?"

"That's where I place my worries, fears and the wounded parts of my soul while I do my work. It allows me to stay focused. When I have completed my task I can collect them. Or, perhaps a better description is that I can collect them to indulge once again in irrational beliefs, denial of truth and overwhelming emotions." The woman stood up from her seat. Follin could feel her power, her sharp, crystal-clear mind was awesome.

As the woman's blindfold fell from her eyes, she swung her swords in swift arcs and savage thrusts. Imaginary wisps of black energy fell at her feet.

"Feel my power, the power of the Swords, and remember: without clarity, you will never find the change point in a conversation, argument or negotiation."

Three of Swords

Sadness; a perception of betrayal; grief and loss.

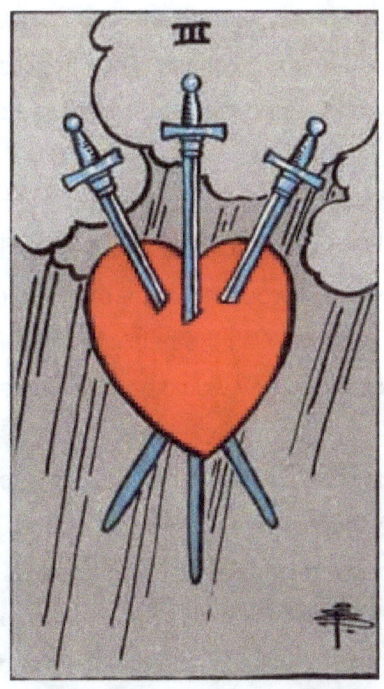

With Sir William's arrival, their trek continued towards the Swords castle through the thick forests and across the grassy plains. The Knight's Swords guard took over the protection of the wagon train allowing Sir Dale and all but a few of his Pentacles patrol to return to their Kingdom, their task completed.

At Sir Dale's suggestion, Sir William took to sending Follin into the forest at intervals with Sox prior to leading the wagon train through the more heavily forested sections on their route.

The Wildlanders in this region were expert woodsmen, they knew the forest ways. They also knew that the goods from the Pentacles Kingdom would fetch high prices in their own lands. Their raids would disrupt trade between the other kingdoms and thus weaken the Tarot Empire's powerful network of support. This was one of the strategies of the Wildlander mages, to create havoc by disrupting the trade between the kingdoms.

It was Sir William's primary objective to ensure that the Pentacles wagon trains be kept safe from ambush. The supplies they brought were of the highest quality and supported the Swords in the defence of their Kingdom.

The knight took pains to impress upon Follin that his forest work might be the difference between their survival and demise. If Follin was able to discover hidden enemies, it would allow them to avoid, or at the least prepare, for their ambushes. With the help of Follin's forest work, it was hoped that this particular journey would be much safer than their previous ones.

The Mystic Isle lovers now spent nearly all their spare time with Pages Natalie and Arthur. They sang Swords songs, learned to play games like cards, checkers and chess. These games fascinated Eve, but chess, in particular, annoyed Follin. He had tried to explain to Eve that his dyslexia caused him to make simple mistakes and this reminded him of his traumatic school experiences.

"Oh poppy-cock, Follin, there's nothing wrong with your mind, it works as well as everyone else's," argued Eve when he spoke about it one night. "Do you think we don't know about your problems? Why, Natalie and Arthur love it when you make mistakes, that means they win more games," she said laughing at the frown on his face. This did not make Follin feel any better though.

"Don't you understand, Eve, I don't want to make mistakes. I don't want to let others win at my expense. It's humiliating." He angrily shrugged her hand off his shoulder and left their tent to walk with Sox in the forest, to be alone.

He found a comfortable tree to lean against and stared at the bright stars between the leafy branches. Every now and then a cloud would cross the skies. It pitched the forest into a darkness so complete that Follin felt like he was enveloped in a gloom of sadness. If it wasn't for Sox sitting beside him, Follin could imagine himself as a school-age child, crying himself to sleep in his pitch-black room at home. He leaned into Sox's warm body, closed his eyes and fell asleep.

It was during his sleep that he awoke in a dream. He recognised that he was asleep and dreaming too. He was in the astral realm, back at his hermit's cottage.

A voice called to him, he turned to see the Charioteer, Sir Darwyn. They had met some years earlier on his journey through the Tarot Major Arcana.

"Follin, come, sit with me for a while," Sir Darwyn called and motioned with his hand for Follin to sit beside him. *"The sun is shining and the weather is perfect for talking."*

Follin looked around at his sod roofed hermit cottage. It looked much the same as when he was on his first journey through the Tarot Major Arcana but everything appeared brighter. The moss was thick and green on the shadow side at the back, while the sun shone on the front where they were seated.

"I've taken the liberty of boiling water for our tea. The Strength lady left some herbal tea for us, she said that it might help clear your mind." The tea emitted the strong aroma of forest herbs and some strange scented spices. *"It has been quite a while since my horses came charging into your life, remember?"*

"Yes, that was quite a while ago. But, Sir Darwyn, I am dreaming inside your dream aren't I?" The Charioteer nodded and watched as Follin's face broke into a broad smile. *"Great! I thought so, I sometimes visit here in my meditations, but your version is so much more alive than* mine. I can feel that you've added something, there's more energy here, it's really nice."

"Thank you, but we don't have a lot of time for chatter. I wanted to remind you of your convictions. Remember the lessons I spoke to you about? To achieve victory you need to take aim at your goal, remain focused, disciplined and do not give up. You also need to keep your lifestyle lean, your habits simple and avoid excess of any kind. You can do this by harnessing both sides of consciousness, to guide them down the middle path." Sir Darwyn had drawn his chariot with its two horses in the dirt at his feet using his short sword to emphasise his point.

"You worry about your past, but you were just a child back then. You lived in a world that was black, while you were white. Your first journey into the Tarot Empire was a success. The child learned to balance white with black, to harness the active side with the passive side. But right now you are setting yourself up to go backwards on this trip into the Swords Kingdom."

Follin listened, trying to comprehend what the warrior knight meant. He remembered the lady with the Two of Swords, *'listen and seek the key words, they will lead you to the change point.'* As he heard her voice it started to come together.

"Sir Darwyn, I know what's happened to me," he said. "My weakness is that I get lost trying to listen. I forget the start of a sentence, and I worry so much about what I'd just forgotten that I don't pay any attention to the middle or end," Follin explained. "The Swords Pages are intellectual giants compared to me and that forces me to remember my miserable childhood. I don't know how many times I was put into the fool's corner. I fear that I am broken beyond mending."

"Follin, you don't need to go back there. Don't forget that you have done your inner work right here, to rescue that hurt little boy. Healing within your inner world is like driving my chariot. When one horse pulls one way what do I do? I unharness it and retrain it to my commands. You *can do the same with your inner child. He is feeling insecure because of the intellectual games the Swords play so effortlessly. Nurture your inner child because right now he is lost."*

Before he disappeared Sir Darwyn paused, looked at Follin carefully then said, *"Remember this, it will help: Arthur will be fine. Watch for the column of smoke, it will guide you."*

Sox suddenly stiffened causing Follin to wake with a start.

"Sox, what is it? Why did you woke me?" When Follin realised that all was well and that Sox was falling back to sleep, he pondered the meaning of his dream. "But I wonder, what does Sir Darwyn mean by *'watch for smoke'*? That is odd." Just then he heard a voice in his head, it was Molly.

"The forest is speaking, young one. They say the wind has turned and it is time for you to return to your bed."

Follin caught the scent of his wife, Eve, and realised Molly had spoken in senses, not words. It was time he made peace with his wife.

'Ah-ha, so that was why Sox woke me, he sensed Molly wanted to contact me.'

The next day dawned bright and sunny, the clouds that threatened rain during the night were gone. At break of dawn the Swords scouts returned with their reports. They had seen heavy concentrations of Wildlanders waiting for them at the Pentacles River crossings to the north and east. Sir William decided it prudent to head south and thus through the forests of the Wood Elves. There they should be able to cross the River of Cups in safety. The elves were known to hunt down the Wildlanders if they entered their territories.

The Tarot Kingdoms had a respectful peace agreement with the elves in this region. The Wildlanders, fortunately, rarely ventured there without the support of their mages. Sir William knew that when their wagon train crossed the River of Cups they would then come under the protection of the Swords cavalry who patrolled the farmlands between the rivers.

"Follin, Hilltown has a Windmage who knows how to fly those wings I told you about. I hope we get to see one when we get there," said an excited Arthur when he heard that they were heading south towards the Wood Elves' territory.

After several weeks hard slog along the infrequently used forest paths they reached the village of Hilltown. They immediately set up camp on the village common, competing for space with the villager's chickens, goats, sheep and cows.

That afternoon Sir William relaxed with a bunch of noisy cavalrymen playing cards. They would look up every now and then to watch in amusement as Sox played with an invisible Molly. They were dumbfounded as they watched the pup racing about the common, apparently playing by himself. No one could see Molly, the elemental, but they could see Sox. They all thought that he was just an exuberant but crazy fae pup.

Follin enjoyed chatting with Sir William. He noticed that the Swords Knight used his spare time composing poems which he recited endlessly as he rode. When he wasn't writing he was sketching and cataloguing the various plants, insects and animals they came across each day. Where ever he went he took his writing and drawing material. Generally a quiet, solitary man, Sir William nonetheless enjoyed a chat, and a mug of ale or summer wine, each evening by the campfire with his officers.

Sir William called Follin and Arthur over to his campsite to speak with them. "Lads, I've just received reports that the Wildlanders are in numbers in the forest east of here, they must have discovered our detour into the Wood Elf territory. I fear that they have several mages to cast spells protecting them against elven eyes, and arrows. They will no doubt try to prevent us getting our wagon train across the River of Cups and under the safe eyes of our patrols," said the softly spoken knight. "Before we ride out tomorrow, Arthur, I've asked Windmage Otto if he would allow you to fly his wing to check the terrain for signs of the enemy. Follin, I'll need you to go into the deep woods and ask the trees if they know of these Wildlanders. I'll send some of our Bowmen scouts with you."

The two were excited but Arthur was a little apprehensive. "Sir William, I've only been up on a wing a half-dozen times. I'm not very good at it, but I'll do my best," replied Arthur.

"Arthur, I know that you can fly a wing and have excellent eyesight, that's why I chose you. The Windmage will be dropping by to talk with you and he will run you through procedures. Follin, I'll need you to go out before sunrise. Corporal Pope will be your scout and he'll have two Bowmen with him. These are experienced woodsmen. They know how to glide silently through the forests and how to avoid contact with the Wildlanders. Avoid fighting, we just want information."

That afternoon Arthur and Follin met with the Windmage. The wizened old man, leaning on a makeshift crutch, spoke to Arthur in a soft whisper.

"Arthur, I'm sorry that I can't go up in the wing myself, but I had a fall last week and twisted my ankle. I have calculated that it will be a mild day tomorrow, just enough wind to get you aloft and it will keep you up there for as long as you need. My apprentices have overhauled and examined the ropes and we've checked the wing itself. All you need do is prepare your mind and eyes."

Arthur smiled brightly. "Windmage Otto, the last time we did this I was up for so long I nearly froze to death. Is it going to be cold up there in the morning? I have a feeling I might need something more than light-weight shirt and trousers."

Otto nodded. "Yes, yes, it will be a little chilly up there. Right then, wait just a moment while I make some calculations." The old Windmage pulled a sheaf of papers and a much worn pencil stub from an old leather satchel he carried slung over his back. He hurriedly sharped his pencil with a fold-up knife from his pocket then asked Arthur to stand beside him. As he looked Arthur up and down Otto began scribbling down a series of numbers, busily crossing some out and adding more. By the time he had finished his paper was filled with small, spider like formulae, drawings and geometric shapes.

"Yes, if you wear your lightest shoes and a second shirt over the top of your first, I think that would be fine. If it starts to get too cold just signal us and we'll haul you down." This seemed to satisfy the Windmage who carefully placed his pencil and papers back into his much used leather satchel.

That night, while everyone slept, Follin was restless. The message of the Charioteer echoed in his mind. As instructed he meditated and found his inner child sitting outside the hermitage waiting for him. They spent time playing in the dirt, building castles and villages out of sticks and stones. But it wasn't enough to ease the fear in his heart.

Follin went back into his meditation and recalled Sir Darwyn's parting words: *"Arthur will be fine, watch for the column of smoke, it will guide you."* He was certain that it had something to do with his friend's flight tomorrow, and he felt powerless to prevent whatever it was from happening.

"Psst! Follin, wake up, it's time to get moving," called a soft voice. It was the Swords scout, Corporal Pope. "We've no time for eating. I've got water, bread and cheese. We can break our fast while we're walking."

"I'm coming," replied Follin, pulling his boots and forest clothing on. He kissed Eve, who remained asleep, and climbed out of their tent.

"Where's your sword and bow, my lad?" asked Pope, smiling to himself. The two other archers chuckled softly to themselves.

"Oh, hang on." Follin climbed back into the tent and brought out his sword, belt, bow and quiver of arrows. He strapped them on then clicked his tongue to bring Sox to his side.

"Ready," he said.

"Right you are, lad, that extra pair of eyes and a nose of thy fae dog will be most welcome in the darkness of the deep forest," whispered one of the scouts. He stretched his hand down to scratch Sox under the chin.

"Let's go."

The four of them nodded silently to the camp guards as they glided into the pitch black forest, silent as the night breeze.

At first the paths were broad, well-travelled and worn by the townsfolk, but after a half-hour they slipped into the trackless forest itself. The stars disappeared and they could hear the occasional sound of a night animal on the hunt for its meal.

The scouts' walk was hushed, not like Follin's. Even though he had been born and bred beside the forests of the Mystic Isle, his skills were not as refined as those of these Swords Bowmen. Oft-times he kicked a tree root and stumbled. The Bowmen politely paused to give him time to regain his feet before moving off again.

They eventually came to a gully, in the darkness it appeared very deep, and a wariness entered Follin's mind.

"Stop here, please. This is where I need to do my work with the forest," he commanded the Bowman scouts.

Follin bent down and petted Sox, then led him off the faint animal track and in among the trees. *'I need to sit here, with my back against this beech. This fellow reminds me of the one in the mountains when I went looking for my witch-stick,'* he said to himself.

With Sox leaning against him, Follin closed his eyes. It was not as easy as it had been that time in the mountains. He missed Molly, he called for her but she did not answer. In response he heard, or rather sensed her answer - *'I'm busy.'*

Accepting that he had to do this himself, he slid down into a meditative trance deliberately seeking the beech tree's spirit. At the very moment he connected with the beech he felt a sharp pain rip through his chest. It was an axe blade. It struck him, again and again.

'Argh, it hurts,' he groaned silently.

He instinctively switched his awareness away from the pain and tuned into the beech herself. The message he received was of foreign invaders, they were felling trees - the invaders were Wildlanders.

The Wildlanders were building something, a fortress perhaps? Follin pushed further into the sensations coming to him through the tree.

'A fort on a hilltop between here and the Swords farmlands across the River of Cups. It's small but it's right in the path of our wagon train. They seem to be desperate for some reason... they've got fire and pitch, they might burn the forest to force us to leave the wagons...'

Coming back to consciousness Follin sat for a while considering what he'd just experienced.

'There is no way the Wildlanders would set fire to the forest, they're foresters too. They're born to the woods, to the rhythm and rhyme of the seasons, skilled in the ways of the earth, air, fire and water. Why would they do this? Is our wagon train so important?'

Then it hit him. On analysis of the tree's message he sensed that there were Wildlander mages commanding the warriors, and they wanted to destroy the entire Tarot Kingdom.

They heard the screams and then the sounds of movement as people scurried around the wagon train laager on the village common. The returning Bowmen scouts leapt forward encouraging Follin to keep up with them as they raced towards the sounds of panic.

"Run, lad, 'tis something up and we may be able to help," called Corporal Pope as they raced towards the campsite.

They entered the grassed common, dodged past several village cows, then ran in among the soldiers and villagers gathered around Windmage Otto. Some looked upwards at the sky and some climbed the pine trees to peer into the distance.

"What's happened?" cried Follin as he came close enough to see the commotion around the Windmage and his apprentices. Then he noticed that Page Natalie was crying, her face buried in her hands.

"It's Arthur! I knew it!" he said recalling his dream with the Charioteer.

"The rope broke and the boy fell out of the sky," said a woman in the crowd in answer to Follin's question.

Shaking with fear, Follin pushed his way to the Windmage, but the man was in shock. Follin looked around for someone who might help him.

"Lad, get thee here, quickly." It was Frailbones. "'Twas young Page Arthur, got hit by arrows and the wing thing broke. The rope holding it in place broke too. Lad's gone and fallen to the ground somewhere in yon forest. Ye'll be the only one who can find him before the Wildlanders do, ye and the fae Sox." His hand was wrapped around his bow and he looked keenly into Follin's eyes.

It took Follin a few seconds for the information to register. When it did he recalled the words of the Charioteer, then nodded to his friend as he raced across to Sir William gathering his troops together.

Remembering his news of the enemy fort, he quickly blurted it out to the knight.

"The forest has a Wildlander outpost, they've built a fort of sorts between here and the river crossing to our east. They aim to burn us out if they need to."

"A fort? What in damnation?" cried the knight. He called his scouts over. "Corporal Pope, collect your platoon and skirmish forwards and find out exactly where this fort is."

To Sergeant Mills, he said, "get the men-at-arms ready and march out to cover the village approaches. I'll have the cavalry meet the scouts in one hour." He nodded to Corporal Pope who spoke softly to his sergeant to arrange their meeting place. Both knew the area well.

"Sir," said Follin quickly. "I'm going into the forest with Sox to find Arthur, I don't know how long I'll be."

Sir William looked at him for a moment before nodding his assent. He then went to speak with his horsemen. There was so much activity that Follin felt like he had walked into an angry ant's nest.

"What's this? You're not going into the forest alone to find Arthur? You have to take me with you!" stormed Eve. Her face was red and she was angry, an anger brought about by shock and grief.

"No, Eve, I'm going alone, with Sox. I know where Arthur is, I know what to do. Trust me." Follin hugged his wife, leaving her to support a sobbing Natalie on her shoulder. He immediately set off at a jog in the direction the soldiers had pointed.

"Lad be well 'nough, lass. He has yon dog. Aye, he's a brave warrior and he'll find Arthur, have no fears on that. Don't let yer imaginations take nest in thy mind. I'll make sure nay harm comes to him." Frailbones slipped a long knife into his belt, and, with his bow and a quiver of arrows in hand, he set off to follow in Follin's footsteps.

With the morning sun at his back, Frailbones jogged at an energy conserving pace to catch up with his young friend.

Follin's Meditation - Three of Swords

As he jogged through the forest to rescue his friend, Follin found his consciousness split into two. He was running while simultaneously seeing one of his meditation pictures, the Three of Swords.

The picture was of a heart pierced by three swords. As he wondered at what this might mean he felt the pain at the possible loss of his new friend, Arthur. He could sense the pierced heart of the image itself. In a flash of insight he understood that this image aptly illustrated hardship, grief, loss and sadness.

'But what positives might come of this dreadful situation?' he asked himself as he continued along the faint path through the forest.

'Maybe this card is a reminder that I must cut through the emotion of grief and loss, to seek clarity without further emotional clouding? This is much like the lady with the two swords who had to put her emotions behind her so that she could focus on the intellectual change point in her negotiations.'

Follin contemplated this image and the sensations of grief and sadness it raised inside his chest.

'Is it possible to find clarity and direction in the midst of such anguish?' His consciousness reformed as one as he absently noticed that the forest had closed around him yet the birds were singing with a joyousness that warmed his heart.

'Yes, in times of grief perhaps I can seek the deeper meaning behind the pain. I have just made a friend, Arthur, he is kind, generous and fun to be around. I've never had a friend like this before. I don't want to lose him because I also lose his friendship... but is this all that grief is? Is it just loss of something rather than loss of a valuable human being?'

Follin wrestled with this thought until he melded with the heart itself.

'Humans are emotional beings. Without emotion, love, friendship, hope, humour and all those other things that reside in my heart, I would be just a shell, a nothingness.'

At that moment a gentle, yet authoritative female voice spoke in his mind.

'Follin, some people believe that humans can think their problems away. Us Swords sometimes fail to recognise the power of our emotions to dictate our thoughts and actions. Sometimes worrying thoughts develop into panic or we fear losing something or someone. Thus we grieve before anything has actually happened. Clarity comes in finding the balance between your emotions and thoughts. Please, keep it simple and don't overthink everything which can turn it into more than it truly is.' As the voice ceased he briefly saw the image of a Queen. She appeared as thin as a sword blade surrounded by an aura of kindliness wrapped in wisdom.

As the forest closed in on him a tree branch slapped him in the face. The stinging sensation swiftly brought him back to full awareness.

'I think I need to focus on saving Arthur, that is my lesson with this picture,' Follin concluded.

Four of Swords

Contemplation; heal, forgive and recuperate.

Deep within the forest the over-hanging branches and thick canopy of leaves above screened out most of the morning sunlight. As he ran along the faint animal paths Follin recalled Sir Darwyn's message: *'Arthur will be fine, look at the skies and find the smoke, it will guide you'*.

Follin paused beside a tall pine to catch his breath. He stopped breathing for a moment when he heard the soft footfalls of someone approaching from behind. Sox's ears pricked up and he sniffed the air, then settled and gave a soft whine of pleasure.

"What is it, Sox? A friend?" asked Follin as he quickly drew his sword.

The figure of Frailbones soon appeared from among the bushes jogging towards him. Follin smiled in recognition but at the same time felt annoyance. This was now complicated; he had to protect an old man as well as find and rescue Arthur who no doubt was injured in the fall.

Frailbones was winded, his thin, lean frame bent over as he caught his breath. "Aye, lad... you run like the wind in this forest... you're like... one of them Swords Bowman scouts now, hey." He breathed deeply then stood straight as he recovered his wind. "Sometimes, lad, even the bravest need a back-up, a friend. I'm with thee and I'll cover thy back when we find Arthur."

Follin suddenly realised that he had run off without thinking. Of course he'd need help, Sox certainly couldn't carry Arthur.

"Thanks, Frailbones, I forgot my common sense running off like this." Follin bent to lay his bow, quiver and sword beside the tree. "I'm going to climb this tree to try and see where Arthur fell. I need to look for a column of smoke," he said not thinking that Frailbones wasn't part of his conversation with Sir Darwyn.

"Sure, lad, I'll guard these for thee, me 'n Sox 'ere," said the old man squatting on his haunches as he petted the fae pup.

Follin recalled how escaping into the highest branches of the trees was one of the few pleasures of his childhood. When he was bullied and beaten in class he would escape to the back of the schoolyard and climb the large forest firs. There he would sit and sway with the wind. Up there he could watch the birds nesting and their chicks hatching. He learned about the cycles of nature in those fir trees. He felt that same sense of familiarity now, easily finding branches and footholds as he climbed lightly to the very top.

Holding to the fir branches with his feet and knees, Follin pushed the last of the fine-needled branches from his face and peered around. He had fortunately chosen the tallest tree on a small hill. He could see where the enemy must be building their wooden fortress in a small clearing of felled trees way off in the distance. Smoke billowed where the Wildlander's fires burned.

As he turned to scan the forest another plume of smoke caught his attention. It appeared to come from a single campfire. It looked to Follin as though someone had accidentally thrown some dry leaves onto their fire. This caused it to burst into flame and send a thin column of smoke, like a beacon, into the air. Within seconds the smoke disappeared as the woodsmen must have quickly covered the flames to hide their presence. Follin was certain that this was the smoke Sir Darwyn had spoken of.

When Follin reached the ground he spoke to Frailbones. "I saw a column of smoke, like a campfire was out of control for but a brief moment, then it disappeared. It isn't too far away. We need to be quiet and careful. I'll lead with Sox."

The two crept silently in the direction Follin had seen the smoke. After a short period of inching through the thick underbrush, they heard voices, soft but distinct. Wildlanders spoke the same language as the Tarot Empire, Follin realised, though they did have a strange, distinctive accent.

"Lad, 'tis the Wildlanders from yon Hindamar highlands. I know this dialect, I spent much of my youth working on their farms. That's when I was learning the wagon trade. I worked as a wagoneer there, building and repairing wagons." Frailbones smiled to himself, recalling those far off peaceful times.

"Frailbones, let's see if Arthur is there." His companion nocked an arrow to his bow string, then followed him to the edge of the small clearing.

They saw a band of Wildlanders, six in number with a mage instructing them. They were preparing to leave the scene, each armed with sword and bow. Arthur was on a stretcher which was being hitched behind a horse. The Swords Page appeared to be asleep, or unconscious, and his arm was wrapped in what appeared to be a splint and bandage.

Follin studied the scene for a moment then whispered to Frailbones. "It looks like they are taking Arthur away."

Follin was uncertain, six archers plus a mage. This was clearly beyond his capacity to rescue his friend. He recognised that Arthur could easily be used as ransom for the wagon train.

"Lad, let me approach them. I know this dialect, they may be friends of mine from long ago," said the old man.

"But what if they aren't?" asked Follin, he rubbed at his sweating forehead.

"Then ye'll find out quick like. But fear not, there be a code among archers, even those of the Wildlands. I was one, for a time. They'll not kill thee if you approach in peace. No one likes an arrow in the back so they'll respect our direct and honourable approach." Frailbones began to walk towards the sounds of the archers, Sox and Follin followed behind.

The old man didn't stop at the edge of the clearing but announced his presence while walking into the clearing itself. Follin noticed that the archer band all wore soft, brown leather caps. They appeared calm and yet resolute in their stance and manner.

"Hale and well-met, young Snowy. I heard thy voice and thought it was thee," Frailbones called as his greeting.

Seven heads swung towards the visitors and one, the youngest, a teenager, immediately nocked an arrow to his bow. The man standing beside him saw and pushed his bow-arm down.

"Tis ill-mannered to raise thy weapon at a visitor, especially one whom we know." The man who spoke was middle-aged, balding and bearded. "Hale and well-met to thee old friend. What brings thee to this part of the forest?"

The other Wildlander archers rested their bows on the ground and watched. None seemed bothered that there were two armed men and their dog now standing before them.

The leader of the band of archers, Drevin, stepped forward and said, "Frailbones, well-met my friend, my old granduncle still speaks of your adventures. I see thee has a fae dog and a young'n with you. I pray thee are here for a cup of our fresh brew and some food? Because if yer not, we'll be seeing thy back."

"Drevin, grandson of my friend, 'tis yon injured lad in thy stretcher we've come to fetch. His wife saw him fall and she is grieving bad." The old man looked at the pot of tea on the ground and scraps of a meal yet to be eaten. "Aye, that brew and food smells good. We can eat while we talk, if that be to thy liking."

Abruptly, as though he feared that he had been slighted, the mage stood up from where he had been squatting beside Arthur, and made his presence known.

"Boys, this is not a time for tea and cakes! These are our enemy and you will kill them, now!" he ordered, his voice firm and authoritative.

The same young archer, Londar, moved towards Follin and Frailbones. He put his hand to his sword hilt but froze at the firm voice beside him.

"Have thee forgotten thy manners so soon, son? These be archers of the glen, our welcome guests and fire-mates. Ye'll not listen to the mage, his code of honour be different to ours." The boy's father, Jordan, pulled an arrow from his quiver and set it to his own bowstring. His next words were firm and loud in the forest clearing. "And I'll remind thee, Mage Armitar, ye are but our guest. Say the next word and I'll put the first arrow into thee."

Snowy immediately spoke in support of his friend, Jordan. "And I'll put the second." He too nocked an arrow to his bow. The other archers moved to stand with the two men.

"Sorry, Da, I was forgetful." The embarrassed youth turned to the mage. "Mage Armitar, it not be our code to invite guests to our fire only to kill them. That may be law where ye come from, but not among us

Brown-cap archers of the Hindamar highlands." The teenager now proudly stood beside his father, shoulder to shoulder.

Mumbling to himself the mage backed down but remained beside Arthur's wooden stretcher.

"I expect thee wants to leave now, Mage Armitar, and leave thy hand off thy horse's bridle." Drevin raised his bow and pulled until the arrow's feathers touched his ear. The sudden creaking of the drawn bowstring made the mage turn his head towards the group. His face abruptly twisted into fear and disbelief.

"Archers!" the mage spat and his face twisted itself into a mask of anger. "I'll have your ears to decorate my neck when you get back to camp tonight." He grabbed at his staff, looked intently at Follin and Frailbones, then at Sox.

All this time Sox had been silent, standing quietly beside his master, but when the mage stared at him the pup let out a low growl. The startled mage leapt backwards, tripped, and fell to the ground. The archers all laughed, but Follin's eyes grew wide in fear. In that single moment, the mage let his mental guard down. It opened a portal into his mind allowing Follin to look within.

"Sirs, this mage is planning to bring his men back here to kill you," said Follin quickly. "He will kill Arthur first, and then you six, and finally Frailbones and myself. My dog will be slaughtered and roasted for his meal."

Drevin turned to look at Follin then at Frailbones, who nodded. Quickly stepping over Arthur's still body the Brown-caps leader placed his foot on the mage's cloak.

"'Tis murder thee plans as payment? Why, Mage Armitar, our fee was to be in gold, not in blood. I'll have thy wand-stick and thy cloak before ye leave, and I'll keep thy boots for good measure. They hold thy evil so I expect we'll need to burn them." Drevin laughed with his archer friends as he pulled on the cloak just as the mage stood.

"You ruffian filth! I should turn you all into toads right now!" The mage's voice suddenly softened. It became a crooning, soothing sound that had the effect of calming the tension between himself and the archers. Follin suddenly felt strangely safe and friendly towards the mage. "I promise to pay your fee of gold when you bring this lad and his two friends, back to our camp. I'll leave you to have your friendly cup of tea and to chat with your visitors. I look forward to seeing you all tonight for your payment."

The mage stood and pulled his cloak from the archer's limp hand, there was no resistance. Each member of the band looked at the mage as though they had rudely insulted him. Right at the moment the archer's faces softened, Sox barked loudly. It brought everyone back from under the mage's spell.

Drevin, realising that he no longer held the mage's cloak, now reached forward to grab it again. He then roughly pushed the mage to the ground.

"Scoundrel! Ye had us magicked you did." Turning to Snowy, Drevin gruffly ordered him to take the mage's shoes and staff. "Ye struggle and ye'll feel this blade between thy ribs. Us Brown-caps won't be tricked again by thy mealy mouth, once tricked never twice. Us folk of the Hindamar highlands never forget a face nor a bad deed done against them or theirs." With a kick to his rump the mage was sent to limp barefooted along the faint deer path, back to the Wildlander's new fortress. The group could hear his curses for some time afterwards as he stumbled from one sharp rock to the next.

Follin turned to the archer who had spoken.

"Drevin, thank you, but that was so strange. I knew he was evil but at the same time I felt I owed him a kindness."

"Aye, but don't thank me, lad, 'twas thy dog what saved us. If thy dog hadn't broke the mage's spell we'd have been lying dead beside the boy here in the sled. Mages can trick us mountain men once, but that be his last."

Drevin sat down beside the fire and nodded for the younger members to open their packs and bring out their clay mugs. Together they drank the hot tea to old, but not forgotten times. The mage's boots, staff and cloak burned in the fire as they talked.

Follin absently patted Sox as he enjoyed the strange flavour of the men's tea. They explained that it came from a special shrub high in the Hindamar Mountains. He opened his pockets and brought out an apple he'd forgotten and offered it to his hosts.

"Why, old Frailbones, the lad has manners, ye'll make an archer of him yet," remarked Jordan nodding at Follin's Bowman bow and quiver. "Lad, you be our fire-guest, but since ye have offered thy own food we shall share this among us as your gift. It doesn't matter what clan or kingdom one comes from, an archer is a special breed of warrior. Ye are bonded to us and we to thee. If ever ye need a friend, we be ready to meet that need."

"But what about Arthur, he's our friend and his wife is grieving just as Frailbones said. That's why we're here, Jordan. We would like to take him home if we may," said Follin softly, hopefully.

Drevin was a man of middle years with a strong face and powerful shoulders. "Have no fear, lad, he be our prisoner, we can do what we want with him now. We were promised payment to bring him down and to capture him for that scoundrel magicker, Mage Armitar."

Follin's face dropped. He didn't want to fight these nice men, even though they did hurt his friend. He also knew that if it came to a fight both he and Frailbones would lose and they would no doubt die.

"Son, Drevin is an honest Brown-cap archer of the Hindamar Mountain highlands," said Frailbones trying to help this young Mystic Islander understand the ways of archers. "His father was my good friend, sadly now passed on..."

"But he had a darn good life," interjected Snowy.

"Aye, he did at that," agreed Drevin.

Still, Follin remained confused and worried. Frailbones nodded, understanding.

"Lad, what I'm saying is that we can take Arthur home now. There be no bad blood between us archers." The sounds of approval and agreement came to Follin's ears and he began to relax.

"You mean we can take Arthur home?" he asked.

The man nodded, smiled, then answered. "Lad, if thee and Frailbones says ye wants yer friend, then be it so. Young lad is sorely wounded, and as he be your friend then that makes him our friend." Drevin slapped Follin on the shoulder. "But take care, the lad has a bruised head and a broke arm. Lad was given a sleeping draft by the mage to keep him quiet while we were to take him to the camp. That be just as well, I'd say the fall must have frightened the spirits out of him, and the sudden stop must have hurt some too."

Follin smiled to himself remembering the lesson from Sir Darwyn's friend, the Strength lady with the lion, during his sojourn with the Major Arcana. Sometimes not-doing worked better than doing.

"Thank you, sirs. I'm not quite an archer yet but I want to be. I'm quite good but my strength has yet to improve," explained Follin. "Can I check Arthur now?"

The leader nodded. "Lad, we won't leave until ye are ready. Aye, ye can take yon friend on the stretcher we made. Sadly, we'll need the neddy to carry our own gear. I wish we could be of more help."

"Thank you, you saved Arthur and you stood up for us against the mage, that's help enough," said Follin as he leaned over and began testing Arthur's joints and bones. He noticed his friend's forehead was bruised, cut and swollen. It appeared that he had just the single broken arm and it was already set with a splint by the mage. "Frailbones, it looks like Arthur hit a few tree branches on the way down, he's got some bark splinters in his head."

"It is just as well that pine needles are soft. He must have hit more leaf than bark then," said Snowy as he heaped soil over the campfire. "Come on lads, time we started back to camp. We need to get there before the magicker stirs up trouble. One can never trust a mage, even one without shoes. When we get back to camp we'll be as welcome as a child stepped in a dog turd at a wedding. We'll just get our gear, quiet like, then we'll be heading home. No use us hanging around waiting to be executed by that villainous mage's people."

"Da?" called a nervous Londar, the youngest of the band. He was still a teenager but there was a set to his broad shouldered stance that made him stand out.

"Da?" he called again as they all stood and began packing their cooking gear into their horse's saddle bags.

"Aye, son? What did ye want?" answered his father, Jordan, as he dumped more soil onto the smouldering fire.

"Da, I was wondering if I could help the lad here, you know, when ye head off with neddy back to the campsite. I can stay and help him get his friend back home. I'd like to know that we did something right, now that we know what sort of man that mage be." He paused, "I need to right a wrong. I acted dishonourable, Da."

The youth stood quietly, waiting for his father to respond. The men, who were one moment busily packing, now stood quietly, waiting to hear what the boy's father would say.

Snowy broke the silence to speak first. "'Tis dangerous, lad. Those Swords and Pentacles are a most formidable enemy. Swords archers, them Bowmen, are as good as us, ye know that for a fact."

The leader of the band, Drevin, spoke too. "Londar, Old Frailbones and the lad are strong enough to carry their friend back to their camp.

Ye'll place thyself in danger. Ye know your mother wouldn't cope if she were to lose another."

Jordan had yet to speak. He well remembered how he was once young and filled with battle honour. So he let the others speak their wisdom first. He waited until they'd all had their say then he spoke.

"Lads," he said to the band of Brown-cap archers. "The spirit of honour sometimes speaks loudest to our youths. If the lad must do then the lad must do." He put his hands on his son's shoulders and looked him firmly in the eye. "Son, if this be what ye need to do, then I'll say nay ag'in thee. Do what be right, then find thy way to Big Rock. We'll meet thee there."

Londar smiled broadly at his father's words. "Da, 'tis what I must do. I couldn't leave our fire-friends to do this task alone, 'twould be wrong. I'll meet thee at the Big Rock."

Follin was more concerned with this turn of events than comfortable. He certainly welcomed the friendship and the help, carrying an injured Arthur would probably prove too much anyway. Arthur was slim but he was solid, it would probably take two days to drag his stretcher back to the village common where their camp was. He was about to speak and thank the band when Frailbones spoke.

"It be on my honour to care for thy boy, Jordan. I remember his mother, ye was a-courting her on one of my visits to thy village. She's a fine woman and the loss of yer eldest would have hurt her deep."

Follin joined Frailbones in shaking hands with everyone in the Brown-cap band. With calls of friendship and well wishes, they went their separate ways.

Follin's Meditation - Four of Swords

In his meditation Follin stood beside a warrior lying on a sarcophagus in a state of deep meditation. His first thought was that this warrior looked very calm and comfortable. He recalled his father once saying that when a warrior returned from battle he often wished to be left alone.

The warrior would spend several days fasting and in meditation and prayer. He would seek peace within himself for the horrible things that he had witnessed; for the horrible things that he had done; and the confused passions that haunted him. It was the warriors way of releasing the hatred, the anger and the horror of war so that he could embrace the calm, gentle nature he needed to return to his family and community. The warrior before him was a fitting metaphor for a warrior recently returned from battle.

As Follin meditated he entered a state of calm. He recalled the many times when he would soak in the bath tub after a particularly tough day at Master Pew's smithy. Many a time he would fall asleep in the bathtub, only waking when the water cooled. That level of calmness was what he now experienced in this meditation.

With a grunt the warrior opened his eyes and sat up to stare at Follin.

"Hello, young seeker, your presence has woken me from my meditations." The warrior yawned and rubbed his tired eyes before continuing. "I can see that you have questions regarding my presence here lying on this sarcophagus. Let me explain. There are three parts to my lesson which I think will help you better understand the Swords Kingdom.

"Firstly, there are times when I must seek to clarify my feelings of revulsion, horror and cowardice that I experienced and witnessed in battle."

"Sir, so this way of meditating is a form of cleansing for the mind? A bit like the other Swords pictures I've meditated with?" asked Follin.

"Yes, in a way it is. Warriors of life can become trapped and tortured by the horrors they experience. For sensitive people like you and I, life experiences can cause severe, lifelong trauma too. These may just as easily be the result of a vicious argument between friends, just as much as a savage fight between enemies in battle. This meditation allows me to create a sanctuary, a structure, to better manage those things that crowd my mind. A warrior of life needs to find peace within, to come to terms with one's confused thoughts thus enabling them to survive."

"Is there no hope for someone, like a soldier returning from battle, to remain whole and happy?" Follin asked.

"A soldier goes into battle to do terrible things, things he would never countenance in his life as a farmer, a cook, a scribe or a servant in the castle. On his return he must release that part of him that is capable of doing violence. He must find a way to embrace his kind and gentle spirit, that part of him that he experiences with his mother, his wife and his children. One part of the soldier's spirit is violent and must do and experience terrible things so as to protect those he loves. But that part of him must not be allowed back into consciousness once he is no longer at war."

The warrior lay back down to resume his contemplative posture. He closed his eyes for a moment before continuing.

"That is what you are witness to this day. I have released the horrors of battle, that madness that grabbed me and made it easy for me to slaughter my enemies. I did terrible things in the heat of battle for which I am ashamed. How could I return to my family with those feelings sitting within my heart? At this moment I am in the process of the second part of your lesson, I am forgiving myself for what I have done and witnessed." The warriors face became a mask of tormented horror, but soon eased, allowing him to continue his explanation.

"As I release the trauma and torment within and I have forgiven myself, I can begin to rebuild my relationship with my kind, gentle spirit. That is the third part of this lesson – rebuilding your gentle spirit."

"What was the first part again?" asked Follin, his face suddenly flushed with embarrassment having forgotten the warrior's lesson points so quickly.

The man smiled and reiterated his lesson. "Son, there are three parts to meditating on the spirit of life and death. The first part is coming to terms with the horrors experienced in life. These form traumatic memories which may arise from witnessing someone being harmed just as much as being the victim of such harm. The second part is forgiveness, forgiving oneself for feeling such pain; the guilt of being the only survivor of a catastrophe; forgiveness for wishing someone else was being bullied instead of yourself. Forgiving oneself is often the hardest of these lessons.

"The third lesson is rebuilding ones gentle and kind spirit. This means that you undertake specific healing methods that you have done many times in your hermitage. I must admit that your inner child healing is much better than what I was taught. I am going to adopt your healing approach when I have completed forgiving myself. In fact, I think that the inner child healing you do is very much a form of forgiveness. I shall now leave you and ponder this in my meditations."

The warrior closed his eyes once more and sighed deeply. Follin took this to be a sign that he wanted Follin to leave.

"Kind sir, thank you for your lessons. I wish you a safe return to your family." With that the image faded and Follin returned to consciousness.

Five of Swords

Conquest; a clever win; arrogance; witnessing dishonour; self-interest.

Follin and his two friends, the aged Frailbones and the young Brown-cap archer, Londar, took turns to pull Arthur's wooden-framed stretcher. It was easiest if one of them scouted the path ahead while the other two took the front end of the stretcher leaving the ends to drag on the ground. The unconscious Page was slung on a blanket between the poles and loosely tied to try to keep him from tipping out.

    Movement became almost impossible in places where the trees grew close together and the forest undergrowth closed in on the narrow path. The stretcher poles caught on rocks and became tangled in bushes, the men tripped and kicked their toes on protruding tree roots. This caused

Arthur to frequently slip from the stretcher and their journey was interrupted by frequent stops to retie him back onto his stretcher.

The midday sun was driving the temperature in the underbrush upwards. It was soon clear that the aged wagoneer was struggling to breathe in the heat. The sudden gasping from Frailbones caused Follin and Londar to immediately take heed and they stopped on the track. Their own breathing was ragged and their throats were dry. At their stopping Frailbones slowly dropped to the ground and leaned his back against a tree.

"I'm blow'd if I remember the track was as bad as this," rasped the aged wagoneer. His knuckles were bloodied from bashing against countless tree-trunks and sharp, thorny branches. "Lads, I need to put the pole down for a bit. I'll be right, just give me a moment to rest up some."

Frailbones closed his eyes and was fast asleep in moments. Follin and Londar looked at each other, their faces tense with concern. They tipped cool water from their leather water-pouches over Frailbones' face and neck and untied his shirt to tip more water over his chest. Both knew that heat stroke was a real danger in this unseasonably hot weather.

Arthur, in the meantime, had woken and was trying to sit up. His head still hurt immensely from the fall and he collapsed back onto his stretcher. Each time Arthur moved Sox leaned across his body to lick his face in sympathy.

The Swords Page eventually managed to sit up and look around. Noticing Frailbones collapsed beside the tree, and the two young men beside him, he called out.

"Hey, Follin, what time is it? I've got to get back to Natalie. She'll be worried that something's happened to me."

"Hi Arthur, you've had a bad knock on the head and your arm's broken. Do you remember anything about your wing-thing crashing?" asked Follin moving over to sit beside the injured Page.

Arthur only then noticed that his arm wouldn't move, it had been immobilised by the mage's splint.

"My arm's broken? Oh, that's why I can't move it. Follin, what happened to me? How did I get here in the forest?" He was clearly unaware of his fall and still recovering from the draft the mage had given him.

"You fell out of the sky, Arthur. The Wildlanders shot your wing down. You fell and hit your head and broke your arm. The Brown-cap archers helped you though. This is Londar, he's helping us get you back to our camp," replied Follin carefully, trying to measure how much Arthur understood.

"Wing? Oh yes, I was flying. Yes, now I remember, it was so wonderful to be free... but then I fell. It was horrible feeling the rope snap and the wing twisting as I came down. I can't remember anything else though," Arthur said quietly, trying to piece the mornings events together.

Londar moved across to Arthur and handed him his water-pouch. "Here, drink this, it be the last of our water. Drink it slowly so ye don't sick it up."

Unfortunately, Arthur was still semi-concussed and he did sick up his water. It meant that not only were they still a days walk from their camp but they had no water for the two sick members of their group.

With the sun beating down on them, Londar took up their pouches and went in search of water. Sox was thirsty too, he understood what Londar was doing so went along to help. Following Sox's lead the archer found a thin trickle of water dripping down a rock face hidden among tall trees and shrubs. He followed the water to a nearby narrow, shallow creek that held pools of clear, sweet water.

While he was gone, Follin decided to make camp and prepare a sparse meal. With two unwell members of their band it seemed a like a good idea.

When Londar returned both Arthur and Frailbones were in slightly better shape. Arthur's broken arm was paining him but otherwise he was curious about Londar and the Brown-cap archers. He asked them to tell him what happened after he fell.

"Arthur," began Londar, clearly wanting to explain his role in his new friend's plight. "We come from the Hindamar highlands, on the north side of the mountains that separate us from the Pentacles Kingdom. We be known as the Brown-caps because we wear these leather caps, see?" Londar took his cap off and handed it to Arthur for him to examine. "They keep us warm in the cold. We were told by our mage, Mage Armitar, to form a band and head off to the Blue-beard's clan village. Them lads have been at war with the Wands Kingdom for years.

"The Blue-beards are fine folk but they're under pressure from the Outlanders who steal cattle, sheep and even the womenfolk. Ye Tarot Empire lads nay understand what's happening beyond the mountains to yer north. It's much worse than here. We've had skirmishes, fights, stealing and killing, lots of it." Londar looked to Frailbones who was now awake. "Our village is where Frailbones stayed when he was a lad. Aye, Frailbones was right popular too, he could shoot, fight and swing an axe like any of the others. My Da and Uncle Snowy were just kids when Frailbones left to go adventuring. My grandda often spoke of this proud wagoneer, a Pentacles fellow called 'Frailbones'. They said that he was always breaking something, like a finger or an arm." Londar politely stopped speaking when he noticed that Frailbones wanted to speak.

"Aye, as a wee lad I couldn't do anything without breaking me bones." The old man drank deeply from Londar's proffered water pouch, coughed twice then settled back against the tree. "Fingers, arms, legs and everything else. Seems I spent most of my youth with a break somewheres. After living with the Brown-caps for a time I wandered up and down the countryside searching for a remedy for me aches and pains. I found it, but it cost me many years of searching. And do you know what, I found it inside of me." The old man stopped talking as he fought to catch his breath again.

"What did you learn that stopped your bones from breaking?" asked Follin sipping from the other water pouch Londar had filled for them.

"I knew ye'd ask that," answered their old friend. "I was camping up in the mountains one spring when I was met by an old-timer. He just appeared one day, out of the blue it was. We sat and drank tea that he made at my fire. A strange old fellow. He said that I needed to slow down and stop trying to be a man, to let myself grow into one. I thought that was a rather strange thing to say, especially to a young man who had been told to '*grow up and be a man*,' all his life."

Follin frowned. "Was that man you met called The Hierophant?"

Frailbones looked carefully at Follin and smiled. "Aye, 'tis the same. I've met him but a few times and on each visit he had a different name and different guise. But I suspect he be the same man."

Arthur had recovered and was now able to hold his water down. "Frailbones, what did he teach you? What was it that could heal your bones?"

"Lad, The Hierophant showed me this technique. I refined my method with the help of several other wise ones, and the Wood Elves here about. I eventually managed to heal my breaks and strengthen my bones." Frailbones stopped as the three immediately asked about the mysterious elves.

"One day I'll tell thee about my life with the elves, that story has never been told and today ain't the day I speak it." He paused to drink another mouthful of water. "I'll teach thee the method of healing I learned since you have a bone that needs mending. It's not easy, nor is it too hard for a Swords Page to put the effort into learning."

The three leaned forward waiting expectantly.

Frailbones smiled at them and decided to open up a little more. "That wise old man said that he had lived a long time, perhaps longer than time itself. He said that he had learned much in his wanderings through the lands. He taught me the first exercise and that was to be still within my mind and body. He did that by teaching me to learn how to breathe differently. Instead of breathing air I had to learn to breathe light energy."

Arthur let out an audible breath. "Wow, that sounds like magic. How did you do it?"

"'Twas both simple and hard. I imagined drawing light energy into my bones when I breathed in and when I breathed out again."

The fire was getting low so Londar placed more wood on it. In the gloom of the deep forest it shed a light that highlighted Frailbones' aged features. It made him appear older than time itself reminding Follin of his own meeting with The Hierophant some years previously.

"I'm going to show you. Arthur, give me your good hand," he took Arthur's hand in his, then closed his eyes. The old man began a slow, soft, rhythmic breathing. It slowly became fainter and fainter until there was no visible sign that he was breathing.

Arthur's eyes lit up and he smiled with delight. "I can feel it! I can feel it like warm air flowing through my hand... and it's now moving up my arm and into my broken arm... argh! It sort of hurts but it feels good too... it's now in my wound, where the break must be... it's nice and warm," continued Arthur. The smile on his face reflecting the joy in his words.

Frailbones opened his eyes and adjusted his position to lean against the tree trunk again.

"There lad, that's what it feels like. But the doing is hard work for an old man like me. When ye breathe ye imagine the air coming in, warm like, into your arm then ye can send it anywhere ye need it." Frailbones nodded, he was getting sleepy after such an effort.

"I'm afraid, lads, that after today's carrying and pulling I've exhausted me energy reserves. What I had left I've given to young Arthur. I'm not going to be very fresh and sprightly for a while. After an effort like that I'll need rest. We've a long way to go and we're now handicapped with two of us not being of much use. I'm afraid I may need a little help. But before I fall asleep I want you to do this exercise every day, Arthur. Ten times a day if thee can. Just sit, relax and breathe. The most important thing is to start with yer imagination then slowly it becomes real."

The three youths watched as Frailbones closed his eyes and instantly fell asleep, just as he had earlier. They looked at each other in amazement. What they had just witnessed was magic, and to come from old Frailbones was just too much.

"Well I'll be hog-tied and gagged, did you see what he did? He did magic. I'd never have guessed old Frailbones would be a magicker, ever," exclaimed Arthur.

"Old men sometimes know a thing or two," added Londar. "My grandda said Frailbones was an inquisitive youngster. He'd always wander off until one day he never came back. They wished him well on his journey to find a remedy for his injuries."

"Well, Arthur, are you going to practice it? Because I sure am!" chuckled Follin as he settled beside the fire. He decided that it was best to wait for Frailbones to waken before deciding if they should set off for their camp at Hilltown while they still had daylight.

Within the hour Frailbones was awake. He was quite refreshed and suggested that they should keep moving in case the mage came looking for them with some of his men. Arthur said he could walk but he was still a little unsteady.

Follin knew that Frailbones hadn't fully recovered from pulling Arthur's stretcher in the heat and then giving him his energy. He was now in a conundrum because he needed Londar to help him with both Arthur and Frailbones. The problem was that the closer Londar came to the village and their camp the more danger he was putting him in.

"Londar, we might be able to get to camp by this evening - if we don't have any stops. Do you think you could help us just a little longer?" asked Follin, hopeful Londar would agree.

Before Londar could answer Frailbones spoke in a tired voice. "Follin, Londar has done enough for us, lad. He's paid his debt to Arthur and proven his honour. I'd be uncomfortable placing young lad in danger by taking him any closer to yon camp. Sir William will no doubt already have scouts looking for us. I'd say they are even now following our tracks. If they spy young lad here, they'll kill him, make no mistake of that."

Again, Follin felt confused and awkward. He desperately needed Londar's strength to help bring Arthur and Frailbones safely along the narrow forest paths back to the camp. To continue as the only able-bodied one to care for his two companions disturbed him.

Follin turned to Londar. "I know I am asking you to put yourself in danger if you go any further. I wish I could ask you to leave and meet your Da and friends at the Big Rock, but I need you for but a short time. Is that too much to ask of you?"

Frailbones looked sharply at Follin then deliberately turned to stare steadily at the fire without contributing any more to the conversation. Arthur was similarly quiet as he watched the interactions between the three. He wanted Londar to stay with them too.

Londar thoughtfully considered the request. "Aye, I'll walk ye a little further. My Da would be disappointed if I ran off now without fulfilling my duty to thee." With that he stood and hitched his pack over his shoulders, grabbed at his bow then bent down to help Arthur stand.

"Arthur, lean on me, I'll help thee," he said softly. Arthur smiled up at him and stood, swaying only slightly. Once his dizziness dissipated he was able to walk with one hand on his new-found friend's shoulder.

Follin bent to help Frailbones and could not fail to notice that the old man wouldn't look at him. He could feel Frailbone's shame of being weak and his hurt pride in needing someone to help him walk. He also felt the shame of thinking only of himself and not the safety of their new friend, Londar.

Loaded down with two disabled members the group set off along the faint track heading to their campsite, led by the ever-exuberant pup, Sox.

With Follin gone, Eve was restless and frustrated. Just when they were starting to find a rhythm in their marriage this accident to Arthur had to happen. It threatened to throw their lives into disarray. She was confused and distraught at Arthur's fall, Natalie's tears, and at her own inaction. A girl who prided herself on her ability to act smartly in a crisis, she decided that now was as good a time as any to do something constructive.

"Sergeant Lards!" she called. "Sergeant, I want to do something. I'm useful, I can help, just give me something to do," she pleaded.

The Pentacles sergeant was busy worrying over the many tasks ahead of him, but immediately came out of his reverie when he heard his name.

"I'm sorry, lass, I've been thinking and planning and worrying. There's nought but me to protect the wagons. Even the villagers have scarpered behind their walls. We've camp helpers, cooks, thee and me, lass," he said bleakly.

Eve looked around and saw the camp cooks busy preparing the midday meal; the cavalry squadron's dust cloud fading on the dirt road; Natalie sitting on a camp stool looking like a lost child; and there was just a handful of camp helpers cleaning up the mess left of their troop's hurried breakfast. There were no other soldiers besides Sergeant Lards.

"Oh, I see... where are all the guards? Surely they've not all rushed off to capture the fort leaving us unprotected?" she asked the sergeant.

"Afraid so, lass. There is a squad that is supposed to be back in an hour. They've gone but part way down the road to secure it for the lad's return. It seems the fight at the Wildlander fortress has made everyone forgetful."

"That means just you to protect us if the Wildlander's play a trick and double back and capture or kill us?" said Eve, softly, so that Natalie wouldn't hear.

Sergeant Lards rubbed his chin, then he took his helmet off and wiped his brow. It was an unusually hot day and the sun was starting to pound into his head.

"Seems so, lass. How good can you pull a bow or swing a sword?" he asked half in seriousness.

Eve looked around at the forest edge. The village common held a smattering of milking cows, some beef cattle, sheep and goats. There were chickens too that appeared to prefer the Pentacles' camp to the forest.

"I can't believe we've been left undefended like this. It's so... un-soldier-like," she muttered.

Lards heard her. "Lass, we all make mistakes. It's been a mad morning with Arthur crashing down from his wing thing and then Follin discovering the enemy fort. I'm sure the Swords covering the road have it all under control. If it makes thee happy I'll send one of the kitchen lads off to inform Sergeant Mills, he's covering the road with his men-at-arms and some of their Bowman archers."

Before the sergeant could give his order, a squad of Bowmen appeared, running along the road towards them. Their leader, Corporal Pope, ran over to Sergeant Lards.

Panting hard, Pope made his report. "Sergeant Lards! Sergeant Mills sends his apologies, seems he took everyone available and left the campsite unprotected." Pope stopped then backed up. "Sorry Sergeant, I must amend that. Sergeant Mills sends his apologies, it seems he took everyone bar you which left you alone to protect the campsite," he smiled, disarming the sergeant's terse reply.

"So it seems, Corporal Pope." The Pentacles sergeant couldn't hold back a wan smile from pushing the serious frown from his face. "But it's good to see you boys here with me nonetheless. You have, hmm, seven archers? Yes? Righto, place them in a protective screen and let me know when ye have finished."

The archer set his men to cover the road and forest which served to protect the camp itself. He also sent one to the village and stationed him at the top of their watch tower with a shiny, metal mirror to signal if he saw anyone approaching.

"Well done, lad, I couldna' done better. Now I think it's time to send the camp hands around to give your boys a drink and a feed while we wait." The sergeant walked off to the cook's tent and arranged for the archers to receive refreshments. Some of them had been on the run for several hours, they looked exhausted. This would brighten their mood after being left out of the fight at the enemy fort.

None of this was lost on Eve. She saw that now was an opportunity to ask for an archer to escort her and Natalie to find Arthur and Follin. She knew that Natalie would not settle until she knew for sure what had happened to her partner.

"Sergeant Lards?" she said coyly as she walked into the cook tent with Natalie in tow. "I was wondering if you would lend us girls a brave archer to help us find Follin and Arthur?"

The solidly built Pentacles sergeant was no fool, he'd heard that tone of voice before. "You sound just like my own daughter. Whenever she wants something and there's a chance I'll say no, she puts on the cutesy voice. But since it looks like it will get you out of my hair, and ye'll have a Swords Bowman to protect thee and Page Natalie; and since the lass needs to know what's happened to her man, I'll send you with Mondy. He's from here-abouts, a bright lad and with a want to make sensible decisions. Mind, be back a'fore dark, otherwise Sir William will hold my arms behind my back while I have my head lopped off. These Swords lads wouldn't want any harm coming to their Page."

"Sergeant Lards," sniffed Natalie. "I promise we'll be back. I need to know, that's all. Thank you." She took the sergeant's hand and squeezed.

"Lass, you Swords people are brave and strong. I trust young Mondy to protect you. Besides, Arthur hasn't fallen too far away. I'm surprised that neither our patrol nor Follin has returned with news. Now be off with thee."

Stepping out of the cooks tent Lards called loudly to one of the young Bowman standing watching the road, a plate of steaming porridge in his hand.

"Bowman Mondy!" he called, "protect these lasses with thy life, they be precious to us all."

The lithe, dark-haired Swords archer nodded. "Lasses be safe with me, Sergeant, I'll not let harm come to them," he said.

The Bowman quickly finished his breakfast and led the girls to the cook who gave them each a bag of food and water to carry. He made sure his own hands were free to use his bow and sword.

"Ladies, this be our way in the forests. Ye'll have to do the carrying. I'm sorry 'bout that, but harm may come to us and I'll need me hands to defend thee."

The girls nodded, pleased that the young man was already thinking of their safety, besides, the bags weren't heavy. The girls threw the bags over their shoulders and followed the young man at a slow jog into the forest.

The voices were close and getting closer. Follin immediately lifted his face from the cool mountain stream letting the water drip through his fingers.

"Thunderation! It's a patrol. I recognise that voice, it's Corporal Owens." He immediately leapt up and grabbed the Brown-cap archer boy by the arm. "Londar, grab your gear and get going! Frailbones, you'd better stay there and make sounds of your injury. I want you loud and noisy to disguise Londar's escape. Arthur, you too, make that noise you've been making all day."

Follin hastily shook Londar's hand. "Thank you. You now have friends in the Tarot Empire, we'll not forget you." He pushed the alarmed Browncap youth sending him running into the forest.

The voices were getting louder, in another few seconds they would be on the rise and would easily see Londar escaping. Thinking quicker than he'd ever thought in his life, Follin turned to Sox, sitting patiently at his feet.

"Sox, get to the patrol, bark at them and annoy them. You've got to stop them coming closer or they'll be after Londar, he's our friend." He pushed Sox toward the approaching soldiers. The next moment the three heard barking, the voices rose in response then broke into laughter as they recognised Follin's fae pup.

"Lad," called Frailbones from beside the creek, "that be the fastest I've seen thee move, and think. But ye have put that brave Londar in grave danger. Your folly may cost him his life. It be on thy head and my shame if they see yon lad running through the trees."

Just then the patrol of two Pentacles men-at-arms and two forest-green Swords Bowmen breached the rise and saw the small group sitting by the stream. Arthur and Frailbones both moaned loudly to distract them.

"We've found you at last. How is Arthur, and is that Frailbones groaning too? Come on lads, let's lend a hand." The corporal and his men gathered around the group by the stream. They quickly built a fire to roast some nuts they'd collected while seeking Arthur and boiled their billy for a cup of tea.

"We've missed our lunch we did," one of the Bowmen complained. "We be right famished."

"How much further is the camp?" Arthur asked trying to keep the men from looking into the forest towards Londar's disappearing back.

"It will be a few hours walk, nothing much really," the Pentacles corporal chatted lightly as they sat quietly eating and drinking. "I saw some beautiful timber. I'm planning to take some home to give to my father. He'll turn it into chair legs, mugs and bowls and all sorts of things. Here, grab some of these. The lads collected some hazelnuts... and we saw a walnut tree, loaded it was. But the nuts weren't quite ripe so we had to leave them on the tree. Pity, cook would have made us Walnut Pie."

Only a handful of Pentacles soldiers had remained behind with their wagons. They would return with them to the Pentacles castle once their goods had been delivered.

"We saw some pretty forest birds too," said the other Pentacles man-at-arms, Clayton. "Hey, Page Arthur, what are those red-feathered birds called? They make a hell of a noise, like someone's trying to strangle a cat."

Arthur was feeling a lot brighter, Londar had helped him through the worst of his dizzy spells. "I think that's a Red Crest, we call them 'cat-screamers'. I'm glad we've not got any around our campsite, they start their screaming just before dawn, curse them."

One of the Swords archers, Grim, had been carefully checking the footprints around the muddy stream bank.

"Corporal, there's four pairs of tracks here but only three of the lads. There be footprints of a Wildlander here, looks like that be archer."

The other soldiers stood up and walked across to look. "Yes, definitely Brown-caps. The stiffened leather sole of a mountain woodsman," said the other Bowman, Herschel.

Corporal Owens came back to the fire and sat, he looked carefully at the three seated on the ground. "Lads, there's something funny here. If I didn't know better I'd say you had a helper to carry yon Swords Page." He didn't ask a question but simply made his statement, then waited.

Arthur was about to speak when Follin spoke over him.

"Corporal, it's quite true, we had a young man help us. If you would like I can tell you the tale." He said, knowing this might give Londar more time to escape if the corporal was set on chasing him.

"Now that be a tale we'd like to hear, lad. It will help solve the mystery we have before us," smiled the corporal, though he appeared to be a little more serious than Follin wished.

"Well, it was like this. Frailbones and I found Arthur, but he was surrounded by a mage and a half dozen Brown-cap archers..." Both Arthur and Frailbones added their piece until the tale was told. They made sure to spin the story out to a full hour. Corporal Owens noted each interruption and each repeated segment, and how they all had to tell it in their own particular manner.

"So, yon lad raced off when ye heard our voices? Seems us Pentacles are poor woodsmen. I'd say the lad got away because we were lazy, thinking that we be on a holiday stroll rather than a patrol with an enemy behind every tree." Owens then grinned as he said, "If the lad was honourable enough to stand by his word, brave enough to help a fellow in need, then we need to be honouring that lad too. 'Londar' you say his name is?" The corporal tossed the youth's name around in his head for a moment. "Then if we ever meet the lad we'll be sure to honour him the way he has honoured our friends here."

Owens turned to his men. "Lads, be it known to us and our troops, Pentacles and Swords, Brown-cap youth by name of 'Londar', is Follin and Page Arthur's fire-friend. He's not to be harmed unless he tries to harm one of ours." Turning to Arthur he said, "Page Arthur, is this what ye wants?"

Arthur nodded, quite taken aback by the soldier's words. "Yes, yes, of course, he saved my life, just as Follin said. If it wasn't for Londar and the other archers, that miserable mage would have had me. Then he would have held our whole wagon train hostage. I know Sir William would trade anything for me and Natalie."

"Right, we keep this to us and our own then. I'll speak to the lord and inform him of your story. I'm sure that he will agree that my action was correct. But let me tell it," he looked directly at Follin. "Lad, I know you did the right thing, but sometimes lords can be cantankerous. Leave the explanations to me, OK?"

Follin's Meditation - Five of Swords

The image was of a swordsman collecting several dropped swords and two soldiers walking away from him. It appeared that they had lost a fight and their swords, or were shamed into leaving their swords behind. Follin decided to enter the picture. As he did so he stepped over to the man holding the swords in his arms.

"Sir, I'm confused, what do your actions mean? I see success but also rudeness, a certain pleasure at winning. But there still appears to be a mystery of your actions."

The man turned to look carefully at Follin.

"There is no mystery about this matter, young man. I won the fight and they lost. I was the superior swordsman," the man answered.

"Those men who lost, they don't look happy. They look downhearted as though they were cheated," replied Follin.

"Who cares? I took their surrender, isn't that what being a warrior means?"

Follin considered the man's answers.

"Sir, I wonder, did you trick them?" he asked.

"Aye, I did at that. I had need and they provided me with the means to achieve that need." The man looked seriously at Follin. "A word of advice lad. Sometimes in life a man must act in self-interest. But to do so places enormous responsibility on him. If you are ever in a situation that requires you to use another, do it reasonably, respectfully and responsibly. That is my lesson to thee."

Follin thought for a moment then asked, "Do you mean that in some circumstances I should act in self-interest rather than in honour?"

The man bent to retrieve his swords before answering. "Certainly. What if you are faced with overwhelming odds and you place your family's lives at risk by making the wrong decision? What do you choose to do? Act honourably and your family's lives are snuffed out? Or play a trick on your enemy so that you and your family survive?"

Follin's forehead furrowed as he thought this through. "But sir, how do I know the difference?"

The man hitched the swords together with his leather belt and threw them over his shoulder. "That, my friend, is up to you to decide."

Six of Swords

Change; travel; a strategic move; recovery from a tough situation; escape to or escape from.

Eve, Natalie and the Bowman, Mondy, set out towards the hill where they thought Arthur may have fallen that morning. Eve had watched as Follin and Frailbones rushed off to find Arthur but then the entire camp had erupted into a maelstrom of activity. The soldiers had hurriedly left to attack the Wildlander's fort on the road to the Swords castle, then they were gone. All that was left was the campsite, suddenly silent and unprotected.

As the three entered the forest the young Mystic Isle girl became agitated and disoriented. She asked Mondy to stop so that she could rest.

"I'm sorry, I just feel faint for some reason." Natalie saw that Eve was unsteady on her feet and quickly grabbed her. She eased her friend into a comfortable position at the base of a tree. Mondy didn't quite know what to do so he stood scanning the forest for danger while Natalie tended to Eve.

Once her eyes closed Eve could clearly see the astral forest around them. The first thing she noticed was Molly, sitting on her lap, waiting patiently.

"I thought you'd never notice," said the little elemental. Her blind mole-eyes were closed tight and her tiny ears upright and alert. "I've been calling you all morning. I've even told master Follin I was busy so that I could speak with you," she said. Eve abruptly realised what it was that Molly was trying to convey to her – danger!

"What is it, Molly? What's dangerous?" she asked somewhat alarmed.

"I've been trying to tell you, there's danger out there, here, around you. Some force wants to stop you continuing your journey to the Swords Kingdom." Molly then projected the warning in her sensory manner that Eve still struggled to comprehend.

"Molly, I can't understand your type of messages. You'll have to slow down," she muttered.

Natalie heard her friend speak. "What did you say, Eve? Did you want some water?" she asked, concerned for her friend. Natalie was worried, they had only just left the safety of the camp and already they were in crisis.

"Missus said something about 'slow down' I think," offered Mondy who had come closer to listen to Eve's mutterings.

Molly stopped sending her sensory messages and tried to find a better way to communicate with her mistress. Molly had no vision, she was a simple, blind mole. All she knew was feelings, smells, tastes and sounds. Now she was in a bind, how should she convey the feelings and tastes of danger that she knew Eve was now exposed to?

"I'll communicate the message I received from the trees, that might be closer to what you can understand." As she had done for Follin, Molly put her mind into the trees of the forest and tapped into a stream of consciousness that was of wind, air and the senses of the outside world. Although Molly was of the earth, a dirt burrower, she very much liked the trees. Trees were refreshing and they always had plenty of food for her and her kind. They gave off an aura of security and freedom that other creatures lacked.

Eve had remained in a state of semi-consciousness and quickly caught the messages of the trees.

"Molly, I can feel it, it's so nice, the wind and the smell of leaves and earth, rain and mist, this is beautiful... but there's fear as well, fear of pain and hurt and loss... it's fire! I can see flames leaping upwards, burning the leaves, trees dying... but there's something more here..."

"Eve, my mistress, that is what I've tried to send it to you, but I didn't have senses for it."

Molly went back in time to her wanderings of earlier that morning and sent the message the trees gave her, in the same manner that she had done for Follin. In the tree's message lay an image of a mage of the Wildlanders, hurting trees, then lighting fires. The feelings of the mage were amplified, she felt his lusting for Eve and Follin.

"Eve, it's a force, a power, like Hera and Hermes. It seeks to harm you and Follin. You are a threat to them."

"Now I understand, Molly. I can feel the stress of the trees... they are being burnt alive." Eve shuddered. Natalie and Mondy looked at each other, concerned as the emotions of pain and suffering playing across Eve's face.

"Yes," said Molly, "that's what's happening." Molly stopped sending messages when she noticed that Eve had begun to drift off. *"You need to be careful, the forces against you seek to take you and use you. Get away from here, get to the Swords castle. Arthur and Follin are fine. Now run, but don't go back to your camp, there is danger in that direction."*

Eve suddenly sat up, she opened her eyes and looked around, confused. Why were there no flames or smell of smoke? She saw that the trees swayed gently in the warm breeze, there was no hint of terror or pain. Everything around her was peaceful, just another pleasant day in the forest.

"I saw fires and trees burning, I could smell smoke... we need to leave, we need to get to the Swords castle now," she said.

"What are you talking about?" cried Natalie, "we're supposed to find Arthur!"

"Shhh! Listen!" Mondy said softly, but forcefully. "There's fighting, in our camp, we must go back!"

"No!" cried Eve grabbing at both Natalie and Mondy as she struggled to rise. "There's danger, that was what I just saw. I spoke to my elemental, she said it is dangerous – there is fire and burning. There's also a mage who wants to capture me and Follin."

Her friend, Natalie, and the Bowman archer looked at Eve, they stood frozen, undecided.

"Molly told me that we would meet Arthur and Follin. They're OK, they're fine," she continued.

Just then the breeze blew strongly into their faces and they caught a whiff of smoke.

"Fire!" cried Mondy. They saw smoke billowing amid flames rising above the trees in the direction of their camp. He pulled at the girls and grabbed for his bow and backpack all in one fluid movement. "Get your bags and follow me, quickly, before the flames reach us."

While Sir William was waging war against the Wildlander fort blocking the road to the Swords castle, a small band of Wildlanders and one of their mages, had crept to the very edge of the wagon laager on the village common.

The Wildlanders often attacked weakened, sparsely defended wagon trains hoping to steal some of the goods stored within. Pentacles goods were of the highest quality and would fetch a high price in any market. This attack appeared to be just another attempt to steal food and other Pentacles produce.

Sergeant Lards and his camp helpers formed a fighting front and managed to push the enemy back from the wagons. This gave the archers the opportunity to score hits among the Wildlanders. Within but a half minute the rain of Bowmen arrows forced the small band of marauders to break their attack. They ran for their lives chased by the archer's angry missiles.

"Sergeant, did you notice that there was a mage with them? Now that is strange, they certainly had the numbers to steal at least one of the wagons," mused Corporal Pope. His face glowed red with effort, his fingers raw and bloodied from pulling his bow string with a cut finger. "I don't like this one bit, Sergeant. A mage, a small skirmish without any will behind it, no, there's something wrong here."

"It's lucky we have the wagons in a laager too... hold on..." Sergeant Lards sniffed the air.

"Smoke! It's a forest fire!" As he scanned the area he noticed that the archer lookout in the village tower was frantically signalling the camp with his mirror. Immediately everyone turned to their leader.

"On me!" roared the Pentacles sergeant. "We will hitch the horses to the wagons and get them into the safety of the village." The wind picked up at that moment and hurled a wall of flames at the defenders.

"Well lads, it's time we headed back to camp, Sir William will be annoyed if we're late," said Corporal Owens. He squinted at the sun through the branches. "We'll be there just on dark if we hurry."

They hadn't gone more than a hundred yards when a gust of wind brought the smell of a forest-fire to their nostrils. Sox's ears pricked up at the scent and he pushed close in by his master's side.

"Forest fire!" called Frailbones. "We best be getting into the stream down there. The understory around here is tinder-dry, we be roasted if we don't move now."

The fire front was moving fast. With a gale-force wind behind it the smoke grew thick as the fire sought to consume the humans in its flaming maul. The small group jumped into the stream in time to huddle as deeply as possible in the shallow water just as the wall of flame hit them. There was a slight rocky overhang that managed to protect them from the full blast of the fires incandescent heat.

The blistering heat and flames leapt from the lower undergrowth into the tree tops and then leaped to the next ridge. It spared their stream but dropped a shower of burning cinders onto everyone below.

Follin had reflexively pulled Sox into the protection of his coat as he forced himself and his pup under the water. Sox recognised the danger above and knew not to struggle.

Once the fire front had passed the Pentacles man-at-arms, Private Clayton, crawled slowly from the stream bed and sat on the ground, his body shaking. He stared above at the flaming trees and coughed as gusts of blinding smoke blew into his face. He didn't speak, he simply couldn't. His shocked look was reflected in everyone's faces.

"Pozzleblitz, but that was close," he whispered. "I thought we was going to die then. The sound was like a crashing castle tower, like..." he couldn't find words to describe the sheer wall of sound made by the flames leaping from tree to tree above them.

The radiant heat burned and blistered what skin remained exposed above the water. Huddled beside the stream they watched as a tree limb, wreathed in flames, came crashing to the ground only a few yards away. Some burning limbs fell into the narrow stream itself, hissing and steaming as though in pain. The smoke around them cleared somewhat as the fire roared past their gully in its insatiable greed for more fuel.

"Now that be a story to earn a mug of ale in your old age," muttered Frailbones. The back of one of his hands was blistered and he shook as he tried to sit up.

Corporal Owens looked around and summed up the situation.

"Lads, we might sit here a while, patch ourselves up and wait it out some. Those trees and shrubs on our track back to the camp will still be burning for a while. We might just put a brew on and get some grub into us, we're not quite ready for fire walking just yet." He spoke in a hushed tone as though the silence that remained was too sacred to spoil with human speech.

Though they were now safe, Arthur, Follin and Frailbones remained deeply worried: '*Are Eve, Natalie and their other friends safe?*'

"Ladies, come, quickly! Follow me, keep up and we'll make the safety of the cave, it's not too far." Mondy scanned left and right as he hurried the girls into the forest, racing across the fire front only to be confronted by a wall of rock.

With a loud sigh of relief, Mondy noted that they had made it to the cliff face, but the fire was too close. They were sure to be burned to ashes when the flames threw themselves against the rock wall.

But there, between the gale force gusts of smoke and flying embers, they could see a narrow crevice in the wall of rock. Mondy grabbed the frightened girls and pushed them forward.

"Here, quickly, run into the cave, as far as you can go!" Mondy was now yelling. The roar of the flames and the piercing screams of horses and the village livestock trapped on the common, threatened to overwhelm their minds with terror.

Just as a wall of flame hit the cliff face the small group reached the cave entrance and were thrown inside by its blast of super-heated air and smoke. The girls were flung to the ground, coughing, trying to suck in enough oxygen to stay alive. By putting their mouths close to the ground and breathing between gusts of smoke, they managed to crawl safely to the back of the cave. The roar of the forest fire was so loud that they had completely forgotten of their task to find Arthur - the spectacle of the disaster had stolen their attention.

It seemed like forever but eventually the flames passed. The forest fuel, which had fallen around the cave mouth, was finally consumed. Mondy now looked around and saw the girls curled up together at the end of their tiny cave sanctuary.

"It's finished now," he coughed. "I think it best we wait here 'till sunrise tomorrow. It's too dangerous to go outside before then."

He made his way to where the girls were crouched and sat with them. The three were dazed, their minds shattered by the horror of the sudden, shocking forest fire. They lacked even the volition to reach into their packs to drink from their water-pouches.

Mondy finally shook himself out of his malaise and moved. He passed his water-pouch to the girls.

"This will help wash the smoke from your throats," he whispered in the stillness that always occurs after a forest fire as destructive as this had been.

Follin's Meditation – Six of Swords

Follin stared at the picture of a man polling a boat which contained a woman and a small child sitting in front of him. With the image fixed in his mind Follin stepped into the canoe and faced the occupants.

"Good day to you all," he announced. "Do you mind if I ask what you are running away from? Or is it that you are heading towards something?"

The woman wrapped in a cloak with her arm around a small child answered. "We seek to escape a hardship that we are unable to bear."

The man polling the canoe offered further explanation. "I'm taking this lass and her bairn to safety. They seek a better life, less hardship and perhaps will find happiness and contentment."

Follin was now confused, they were both running away and running towards.

"Dear sir and madam, I'm confused. Which is it? Are you escaping something bad or seeking something wonderful?" Follin tried again.

"Lad, the best thing you can do is to look at the context of what happened before and what may happen after this single event in time. Use your gift of observation, use it to cut through illusion in your quest for clarity. Look to my right, what do you see? Now look to my left, what do you see?"

"On your right there are waves, perhaps that side represents difficulty and hardship? On the other side, the wider side, it's calm and peaceful. Maybe you are steering a course between the two? Maybe, on the one hand, things have been difficult, and on the other things are pleasant... but I'm still confused." Follin moved but quickly froze fearing that he would tip the canoe over.

"Lad, 'tis simple, seek clarity by observing the context in which the information is given. The mists of confusion will lift once you take the time to observe and consider all the pieces of this puzzle."

"Sir, does that mean that myself and my companions are running towards or away from something?" Follin was seeking insight into their current dilemma too.

"Lad, seek clarity through observation. What has just happened? You've almost been killed in a fire. Where did that fire come from? Was it deliberately lit? Was it sent to kill you or your comrades? What mission are you on? What is your greater mission? What other information need you to consider that will help answer this dilemma before you?"

"Ah-ha, I now see that I need to consider possibilities, instead of focusing on the tree I need to look at the forest," replied Follin smiling in wonder at this insight.

"Exactly, this image directs you to observe that which is happening around the questioner. It is not of itself an answer. You gain clarity from the many observable points of reference that are given you. You must then deduct the direction of movement yourself. Now go back to consciousness and process why you have almost been consumed by this fire."

The canoe-man disappeared as Follin returned to wakefulness.

Seven of Swords

Deliberately stealing or taking winnings; entitlement; unearned rewards; wining by stealth; a strategic manoeuvre; ninja activity; acting alone.

Both Mystic Islanders spent the night with their respective groups of survivors. Arthur and Follin sat beside their campfire, talking while the others slept. The smell of smoke and charred timber drifted on the night breeze.

"I wonder how Londar is doing, I hope he didn't get caught in the forest fire," whispered Arthur.

"I have a feeling he escaped. I'd meditate on it and check but I'm afraid all I'll pick up is the pain and suffering of the burnt trees," replied Follin as he shifted to support his weight on his elbow.

"Follin, I'd like to know how Natalie is, too. Did she get caught up in the forest fire?"

"OK, but don't be disappointed if I can't do it, it isn't always that easy you know." Follin was quietly pleased that his friend believed in him, it was validation and a genuine boost to his confidence.

Follin shifted his weight and rolled onto his back. As he closed his eyes he started a slow, deep breathing cycle to enter a light trance. He then sent his mind out to the forest but immediately withdrew. The shock of pain and suffering was too raw, it hurt. He felt the tree's raw pain as they showed him the flames racing up their trunks to whip their branches and leaves into burning embers.

"Follin? Are you all right?" asked Arthur softly, touching his friend's shoulder.

Follin came back just enough to reply. "Yes, I'm fine, thanks. It did hurt, the trees are in terrible pain and they're sad for their friends who died in the fire. But I'll try to go back in."

He was successful and returned to his deep state of trance to sit outside his astral hermitage, thinking of how best to approach this problem.

'If I ask the trees I'll be pushed back to consciousness. If I ask Molly sho'll probably be feeling much the same, she's sensitive to her friends of the forest. Maybe I could ask one of the archetypes?' As he contemplated his dilemma, the King and Queen of Swords appeared.

"We thought you might need some help, Follin, how may we be of service to you and your companions?" asked the King of Swords. He was tall with long black hair and he had an archer's broad shoulders. Follin was struck by the King's sharp, intelligent eyes.

The Queen, standing beside her partner, was of similar appearance, but she was thin where the King was powerfully built. And there was something familiar about the Queen too. She reminded Follin of someone he had recently met. It was her direct but soft manner that caused Follin to remember where he had met her.

"Your Majesty, you helped me in my meditation when I was running along the path to find Arthur. I would like to thank you for your lesson."

Turning to address them both Follin said, "I am sorry I haven't contacted you earlier, but I am delighted to meet you in this time of crisis."

Follin bowed low before announcing the cause of his dilemma. "Arthur and I have a friend, Londar, who may have been caught up in the forest fire, we think he escaped, at least my instincts tell me so. But when I try to ask the forest I just feel pain and sadness."

The Queen nodded slowly before speaking, her voice was soft yet firm and authoritative. "Your wife, Eve, and Natalie are safe, as too is your friend, Londar. The wind shifted and blew back to whence it came. Our Windmages caught the fire before it had destroyed much of our precious forest."

Follin felt enormous relief that everyone had survived, yet he struggled with guilt for placing the young Brown-cap archer in danger.

"My son," said the King, "we know you acted with a degree of dishonour in asking the boy to remain with your group. Frailbones gave his word that he would protect the son of his friend. You disregarded his promise. You may ease your guilt by proving to Frailbones, and to the Brown-caps, that you are worthy of their respect, that your word is your bond of honour. Honour unites a fractured community which is what threatens the Tarot Empire in these troubled times. Honour, Follin, is a gift that you give to yourself. To lose one's honour is to lose one's compass in life."

The words the King spoke pierced Follin's psychic armour. Having his shameful act laid bare before him was worse than suffering the forest's pain.

"Is there no hope for me, Your Majesties? I should have thought of this before asking Londar to stay and help me," Follin groaned placing his face in his hands.

The Queen spoke softly, her voice a gentle balm to his soul. "Follin, you asked Londar for help, he gave it to you willingly. That is not what has dishonoured you. Your thoughts were for Arthur and Frailbones' welfare. If Londar hadn't been there to help, you would all have perished in the fire. I know this for I have seen it." The Queen shared an image of their charred bones not far from their campfire.

The King continued. "The shame you feel is how you so readily dismissed your friend's solemn promise, you dishonoured Frailbones. That is your source of shame. It rests on the remains of your childhood wounds, but it is not of them. Your challenge is to face your shame. Speak with Frailbones, tell him of how you disregarded his promise. Frailbones would rather have died in the fire than jeopardise his honour. You would rather save your friends lives than keep yours. Which is the more valued? A friend's life or one's honour?"

"Before we leave we must warn you that the Wildlander mages are trying to locate you," said the Queen.

Follin awoke with the birds calling to each other, no doubt checking to see which friends and family had survived the fire. It wasn't until breakfast was called that Follin left his contemplation of the Queen's warning during his night's meditation.

Arthur was already up and collecting firewood, at least the wood that hadn't been consumed in the forest fire. He didn't appear to be in too much pain from his broken arm as he sat warming himself by the campfire.

"I see that you are back from where your mind had taken you this past hour." Arthur smiled to show he was not making fun of his friend. "But what happened to you, Follin? Last night, you didn't come back, you just started snoring. I gave up and went to sleep. So, are our wives safe?" inquired Arthur. Follin noted how the Swords Page's usual rapid-fire personality had mellowed, he appeared all the better for his adventures in the forest.

"I met your King and Queen, they said that our wives are safe, they're with one of the Bowmen," Follin said woodenly.

Arthur's face brightened and he sat quietly beside his friend to relish the joy he now felt. Follin didn't say anything else, he just sat quietly as he accepted his mug of tea and hunk of bread.

"Lad be shook-up. I don't think any of us is feeling too bright after yesterday," observed Owens.

"Lad be sitting like that for a while, Corp. He be thinking, maybe doing his magicking for us," offered Private Clayton.

Arthur looked at Follin, trying to get him to join in with the conversation. Follin once more had to force his mind back so that he could commune with his friends.

"I'm sorry, your King and Queen said that Londar, the young Brown-cap archer, made it to safety too." This brought a murmur of approval.

"She also said that the Windmages turned the wind and sent the fire back to where it started. I guess the mages who lit it got what they deserved. I just hope the rest of our people are safe." Follin settled into a more comfortable sitting posture beside the fire and asked for another mug of tea.

"Aye, our Windmages are spectacular aren't they," informed Grim. "They can do fantastical things with wind and currents, as well as fly those wing contraptions."

"Aye, that be so, them fellers can fly without help of a wing. At least that's what I'd heard from me brothers," offered the other Bowman, Herschel.

"Thank goodness your wives and that young lad are safe," said Corporal Owens.

Owens stood and stretched. "One more cuppa and then we're heading back to camp. We've not far to go but it's always treacherous after a forest fire. There will be burn traps, holes where the fire has continued to burn, deep down, following the tree roots. When you step on them you can fall through. I've seen some nasty burns from them burn traps. Just so's we can avoid too much trouble we'll walk in single file. Private Clayton, you take the lead for now, be careful."

Follin felt a shiver of dread pass through him knowing that, with each step, he would feel the forest's pain.

Each member of the group felt the sadness of the forest. For Follin, it was one of almost inconsolable suffering. Fortunately, his pup, Sox, remained by his side, licking his hand when he noticed his master was particularly troubled. Soon his white fur was black from the ashes of the fire to match his black feet.

When they arrived at the village common no-one was there. Several wagons lay as skeletons on the ground, their shapes easily recognisable by their charred remains. There were also a few charred bodies. They saw signs of battle, some arrow shafts remained in some of the bodies, and some Bowman arrows, not consumed by the fire, remained sticking upright in the ground.

———

Eve was dreaming. At first, she was with Molly, walking with her through a forest that no longer existed. Molly was silent and tense making Eve feel confused and extremely uncomfortable. Eve really wanted to ask about Follin and Arthur but didn't think that this was the right time for it.

"Eve, this is the time for grieving. It's what we do, grieving is normal, it helps us heal. Even elementals and non-humans feel sadness and loss," said Hera stepping in front of the two as she sent a wall of love and comfort to embrace them.

"Oh, Hera," sighed Eve, "I really need to know about Follin, is he safe? And has he found Arthur?" She felt a tendril of fear creeping into her inner world. It was alien and disturbing.

"Yes, Eve, they are safe," Hera paused briefly as Eve smiled in relief and embraced her. "But I must remind you that the inner planes can amplify feelings as well as thoughts. You've not been taught to manage feelings in this dimension yet. Indulging in emotions in the inner worlds can do nasty things in the outer world."

Eve suddenly intuited a change in the forest. It was as if a fresh breeze had brought hope and joy to this otherwise barren and forlorn place.

There came a familiar voice, it was The Hierophant. *"You have done fine, young lady. Things are difficult for all in the forest right now. I'd like to take you for a walk, just the two of us. That is if you don't mind?"* he asked. The High Priestess nodded, she had previously invited him to join her for this lesson.

As the two walked through the forest The Hierophant began to speak.

"The forest fire was not an accident, it was intended to drive you and Follin deeper into the forest where several bands of Wildlanders and their mages were waiting. If they failed to catch you they were ordered to kill you."

Eve jumped in fright exclaiming, *"What?! Kill us? What have we done to them?"*

"You are a wild magic that they can't control. For some time there has been a contest between the Tarot Empire and the people that surround it. These people are pressed by their growing populations to find more land and more resources, and so they have decided to take ours. You and Follin are an oddity just like us, the Tarot archetypes, and if they can't manipulate you against us, they will destroy you."

Eve stopped walking and looked at The Hierophant beside her. He appeared as a woodsman, holding a fighting staff and a bright dagger was stuck in his belt.

"What is this you're talking about?" Eve's face furrowed as she tried to understand the enormity of what she had just heard.

"You need to know that the Wildlander mages will be pleased when you are gone from their lands, one way or the other," replied The Hierophant.

"Then how do we protect ourselves? What can we do? Follin and I don't have the same powers as these Wildlander mages." Eve looked around, the scene had changed, she was back in Hera's Sanctuary. Where previously the gardens had shown signs of age and a hint of decay, many of the trees had blossomed and there were pleasant scents and perfumes that awakened Eve's spirit of hope.

"Hera's Sanctuary has sensed your presence and is putting on a display for you. But the amount of energy it needs to do so is enormous. This glade holds our Empire together, it gives us life and purpose, it shines like a beacon to guide and protect our people. The Tarot Empire has been part of this planet for many aeons of time. There are other beings who have crossed this same threshold. If the Empire vanishes,

they will stay, but us...?" The Hierophant spoke softly, touching some of the plants to stroke them gently.

"What happens to us if we lose? Where do we go, where does the Empire vanish to?" asked Eve.

"I've not lived long enough to know that, Eve," explained The Hierophant. *"I've sat with the Emperor and Empress and neither of them know for sure either. The only one who has a foot in both worlds, is Pan, the Earth God. I've spoken to him about this but he said he doesn't know either."*

Follin's Meditation – Seven of Swords

In his meditation Follin saw a young man sneaking away from a camp with a bundle of swords in his arms. It appeared that the swords did not belong to him either. This presented a puzzle that Follin wished to solve. As he pondered the image Follin caught on to some of the picture's meaning.

'This image appears to represent irrational beliefs, denial and fanciful thinking.' He decided to step into the image so that he could speak to the fellow carrying the swords directly.

"Sir, can you please explain to me what is the meaning of your actions?" he asked before the man could run away.

"Oh, hello, I didn't see you there." The man was embarrassed and uneasy. "I've taken these swords because I could. Those people, they have no use for them, they left them lying around to be taken. I might find a use for them one day." The young man rearranged the swords to make carrying them easier.

"But," said Follin, "Isn't that theft? Aren't you just stealing them?"

"And what if it is? Are you going to stop me?" The man became defensive. "I deserve them, they're my trophies, I won them."

'Aha,' considered Follin, 'this is denial, the irrational mind of the Swords. He is not delusional, this is now quite clear. Only someone who can so easily deny their dishonourable behaviour would try to argue that they were doing no wrong.'

Turning to the young man he said, "Thank you, sir, now I understand this lesson. Denial is an irrational justification for a wrongful act. Now that, sir, is the clarity I've been seeking in these Swords images."

The man smiled and adjusted the swords at his back. As he walked off he called over his shoulder, "See, I told you that I deserved them!"

Eight of Swords

A negotiation strategy to appear weak when the path ahead is clear; patience; bound; trapped; caught in a bind; deliberately disengaging from the outside world; an intellectual or emotional binding.

The band of Blue-beard warriors grumbled softly among themselves. Their mage, Mage Armitar, had been pushing them hard leaving no time for food or rest. They were angry for being separated from the warriors sent to harass the Swords wagon train, their faces still displayed some of the paint that they had applied earlier for the battle.

From where they stood it was high enough above the forest for them to see the plains that led to their homelands. The 'Big Rock' they were seeking was at the bottom of the hill. At the crippled mage's command the Wildlander warriors gently set his wicker chair onto the grass.

"Set your trap there," ordered the skinny, surly-eyed mage. "Make sure you kill them all, but leave the boy for me. Just remember it will be your heads on a spike instead of theirs if you fail me."

Mage Armitar had arrived at the Hindamar Mountain villages many years earlier. He had come from the savage clans beyond the Wildlander borders, the Outlands. He was a senior mage and with his band of lesser mages presided over the spiritual ceremonies and cultural rituals of the Hindamar Mountain villages. It was common knowledge, however, that no-one trusted him or his corrupted mage followers.

"Mage Armitar," called Brandar, a tanned, solid warrior, built like a bull. "We have no quarrel with these Brown-caps, you know that. They deserve more for their efforts than to be slaughtered in an ambush by their own kind. It not be honourable."

"Honour?" squealed the mage as he pulled at his bandages to massage balm into his bleeding feet. "Who said anything about giving them honour? Those squibs dishonoured me and by that they dishonour the Mage Guild. Every dishonour deserves punishment and punishment is death. You know this, Brandar. Don't try to tell me that you've forgotten your oath to push the Tarot Empire and their traitors from the face of this land."

"It be dishonourable to us, Mage Armitar, but I doubt you would understand the honour of a Blue-beard of the Hindamar Mountain clans," Brandar said firmly, pulling his shoulders back as he stood over the spider-like mage.

Mage Armitar lowered his gaze then looked at Brandar from within his hooded cape.

"It's for traitors like you that we keep our sacrificial knives sharp," he spat. The group of Blue-beard warriors glanced at their leader. Some stepped back apace and placed their hands on their sword hilts, the two archers quietly nocked an arrow to their bows.

"I'll not touch you, Brandar, but I suggest that you listen when a mage advises you to choose your words wisely. Loose words can only lead to one end and that be tragedy." Mage Armitar had the final word. He turned and waved for his band to pick up his wicker chair and carry him down the hill to set their ambush for the traitorous Brown-cap archers.

"Drevin, it be strange, the forest is too quiet for me liking," whispered Jordan. The archer's leader, one step behind him, nodded in agreement.

"This be strange indeed. One minute the birds are chirping, the next they're on guard," whispered Snowy stringing his bow and pulling an arrow loose from his quiver. The other archers did likewise.

"Peck, go forward, see what's up there to frighten the birds." Drevin now arranged his other archers in a protective screen thirty yards from the Big Rock where they were to meet with Jordan's son, Londar.

"Pst!" came Peck's call as he slid like a shadow back to his troop. He stepped silently over to Drevin. "'Tis Mage Armitar and he's got Brandar and his band of Blue-beard lads with him, two archers. They're setting up an ambush now."

Drevin's face was firm, his lips tight, this was exactly what he had feared, an ambush by Mage Armitar. He knew that mages had magical ways of travel. Even though they had made sure Mage Armitar would struggle to walk in his bare feet, somehow he had managed to get to the Big Rock before them.

Drevin called his men together. "Lads, we've complications. If we push around them, then young Londar will be caught. If we stay here the mage will sense us and send his men to hunt us down. If we ambush them we kill our innocent Blue-beard comrades. Don't forget that Brandar and his men put us up in their own homes when we passed through their village. That makes us fire-friends, we'll not dishonour that bond between brothers."

"Drevin, can't we just talk to them?" whispered Peck. His friends called him the 'silent stalker', a skilled killer of men.

"Peck, sometimes I wonder about you," said Snowy. "I just got a glimpse of that brain it's said you possess."

"Of course we'll talk to them, it's just a matter of how and when," continued Drevin seriously. "But it's that rascal mage I'm worried about. Mage Armitar has out-run us and out-smarted us. He'll use his magic tongue on the Blue-beards and turn them against us. As they say, never underestimate the cunning and the evil blood of a mage."

Jordan spoke next. "Drevin, I see no way out of this, we're already in deep as it is. If the mage gets the chance to magic talk he'll have the Blue-beards into us before we get a chance to negotiate with them. I say we turn the tables on that scab-backed spider and kill him first, then talk to the Blue-beards."

The men looked at each other then slowly nodded in assent. There was now only one thing to do, the dice had been thrown.

"I'll do it," offered Peck, he was their most skilled archer.

"I'll join you, Peck. It's because of my boy that we must do this." Jordan strung his bow and checked the string, then pulled out several arrows to check their shaft and feathers. He chose a particularly well-made arrow for the unpleasant deed.

Drevin silently watched his friends. This was serious business, the execution of a mage would put his entire village to the torch, their families killed and any survivors would be hunted down till they too were eliminated.

"Lads, before we act, know that this will set off a chain of wicked acts against our family and friends. Once thee free thy arrow, we are all dead men and so are our loved ones. We will be cursed to the end of days. Are we in on this together or does anyone wish to pull out now? 'Tis either we are all in on this or we leave and put up a screen to try and save Londar before he gets to the Big Rock and the mage's treachery." Drevin spoke softly but with the authority of his rank.

Again the band of Hindamar highlands archers nodded silently. They well knew the consequences of what they were about to do.

"Lads, this be about honour and the right thing," began Jordan, speaking for the troop. "Mage Armitar be an evil scoundrel if ever there was one. He's done more evil in our mountain village, and that of our neighbours, than any Pentacles, Swords or Wands would ever do. We don't do this for Londar, we don't do this for our own honour, we do this for justice, for our people." His friends nodded in agreement, silently loosening their swords in their scabbards and fingering their bows. They looked to Drevin for the order to begin.

Jordan continued. "Once this be done we shall talk to the Blue-beards and explain to them why we've done it, then we'll parlay with them. Together we'll put things right. If not, then we'll be forced to take our families to the isle, that be the safest place."

At mention of the Mystic Isle, several of the archers placed their right hand across their face to ward off the evil eye.

"All be in agreement with Jordan's words?" asked Drevin, mindful that at any moment the mage would sense their presence and their intention. "Know that the Blue-beards hold jurisdiction for punishment for this crime. If they demand justice, then we be honour-bound to give it them."

Turning to Peck and Jordan he nodded. "Go now, go and set our destiny with thy arrows. If there be blood spilt this day, between Blue-beard and Brown-cap, it be on my shoulders alone."

But still, no-one moved, they waited, bows in hand, arrows nocked, frozen in time. At a final decisive nod from their leader, Peck and Jordan slid silently into the shadows of the forest surrounding the Big Rock.

When Follin and his group arrived at the blackened campsite, there was no one there, even the villagers were gone. There had been a light rain that morning soon after Mondy and the girls had walked through the ashes of their campsite. Their tracks had been erased.

"Grim, you and Herschel run off and check the village. Clayton, you look around here, see what you can find out about what has happened to our people." To their three charges the Pentacles corporal said, "Lad's, we're in a right pickle here. If everyone's dead then we'll be forced to head to the Swords castle without the protection of the cavalry, Bowmen and men-at-arms. With luck they've just been pushed out by the forest fire and we can catch up with them. We'll wait and see what the scouts have to say."

Follin, Arthur and Frailbones looked about but couldn't even find a dry place to sit down. Everywhere was a slushy mess of ash and mud.

"Lads, we'll just have to sit and do our best," said Frailbones. "Follin, you and I can build a fire and put the billy on for tea, maybe cook up some of the soldiers' supplies. This might be our last meal too, so we'll have to tighten our belts from here on in."

"Follin?" asked Arthur, who was feeling much improved. "Did the King and Queen say anything about this?"

Follin looked blankly back at his friend. "No, they didn't. I've not a clue what to do, we'll have to trust our scouts and do what they suggest."

Grim soon returned to squat in front of the warm fire in the cool of the morning air.

"No sign of anyone. The tracks are covered in ash so they must have escaped before the fire got to them. To where they've escaped, I don't know," he told them. By now the others had returned with similar stories.

"The tracks tell us that there was a fight. We can see the Bowman arrows and the bodies, none of them ours. I think the lads were attacked by Wildlanders who then set the forest alight and burned everything. But most of our wagons are missing. Either our fellers took them or the Wildlanders did. Looks like the fire came back upon itself and burned what it didn't finish burning the first time," said Herschel softly.

"Lad, you did say the Windmages turned the fire around and sent it back on the Wildlanders who lit it? That means the fire originated from here abouts and was forced back through the camp and village, they were burned out twice. No wonder they had to run and why just about everything has been lost to the fire," announced Corporal Owens.

"It will take some work to get Hilltown back to the lively place it once was. Nice little village this, good people too. Hardworking, the best brewery this side of the plains..." Grim stopped talking, it hurt too much to remember what was now gone.

Frailbones looked around and saw glum faces. "Come, lads, we've a trek ahead of us, no food and little water. We've got to rely on you lads to get us home safe, especially if there are Wildlanders and their mages about."

Follin noticed how fragile Frailbones sounded. He looked at his aged friend and noticed for the first time that he really had aged since they had left the Pentacles castle. He noticed too, that Sox had been sharing his time between himself and Frailbones.

Corporal Owens lifted his face and continued with his eyes looking upwards at the clouds above. "Wind's dropped and in that direction is the Swords Plains. We've taken this longer route through the forest to avoid contact with the Wildlanders which means we've got a long walk ahead of us to get home."

Owens was brought back to their current situation by Herschel's soft voice. "Corporal, we've the two rivers to cross as well. They be low 'nuff now but still, some of them crossings make for good ambushes."

"Yes, that's something to consider." Owens nodded his head in thought. The rest waited silently, sipping at the hot tea Frailbones had poured for them. "Right, we have two Mountaineer-trained Pentacles and two forester Bowmen. Although Clayton and I don't know this country, our two Bowman certainly do." He looked at Grim and Herschel, waiting for a reply.

"Corporal Owens, we know these parts, Herschel and I be raised not far from here. We be trained on yon Swords Plain and in the elven forests chasing Wildlanders these past few years as well. Aye, we be the ones to lead this expedition." Grim smiled, his crooked teeth were set in a firm but pleasant face. "We'll lead, usual pace, jog one walk one. You be well 'nough to keep up with us, lad?" he challenged Arthur with a cheeky grin.

Arthur spoke smartly in answer. "My arm is healing fine. And, as you should know, Grim, a Swords Page can do anything a ruffian like you can. Let's get started."

Herschel set a pattern of a steady paced jog that led into an energy saving walk to recover. The group continued in this pattern for the rest of the morning only stopping to fill their water bottles at a narrow stream. At midday they stopped again for a rest and drink, then in the afternoon they rested once more. Eventually they left the deep forest which stopped at the bank of the River of Cups. The river crossing was wide but shallow. After careful scouting to make sure it was safe, they waded across to the other side.

All morning Frailbones had grown quieter. His usual positive manner disappeared the closer they came to the River of Cups.

"This be the long plain, and a long walk we have too. We'll meet the Swords River soon enough. The crossing there should be shallow enough to walk across this time of year, much like the Cups one. Not long after we hit the Swords Plains we should be picked up by one of our cavalry patrols. That be if we don't run into a Wildlander patrol first," Grim said as they eased into a walk to relieve some of the pain building up in their fatigued limbs.

He reminded them to keep a steady watch as they travelled. Although the Wildlanders didn't have many horses, only what they had stolen, they were still a menacing presence. Most of the Wildlanders were on foot but they could run, and they had been known to set ambushes in the most unlikely of places.

"What about the mages, what do you think we can do about them?" asked Arthur, mindful of the threat they now posed to Follin and Eve.

"No way to fend them off, lad, that be Follin's job from here on in. We nay have the cover of the deep forest to hide in. When we get to the grasslands we be easily seen. If lad here can magick us some mist or hide us somehow that be the best thing for us," replied Herschel.

"Follin, why don't you try to contact the King and Queen of Swords? They can send a patrol to collect us and our wives," suggested Arthur. The group turned and waited expectantly for Follin to answer.

"I thought of that too, Arthur. I tried to contact Eve last night but was stopped by the King himself. He said that it was much too dangerous. Firstly, he said, it will inform the Wildlander mages of our and Eve's location. He showed me the mage's tapestry of magic which they were using to seek us out, it's like a tightly woven spider web. If I reach out again, even with the King to help us, the mages will find us. I can't risk that. Secondly, the King informed me that help is on its way but when and how I don't know, he had to stop our communication at that point."

The men dropped their gaze to stare at the ground, nodding their heads in understanding. Where they momentarily felt hope they now felt disheartened.

"What about your cavalry patrols, won't they be patrolling the plains looking for those scattered by the forest fire?" asked Corporal Owens.

Grim and Herschel looked at each other and silently nodded.

"Yes, I'm sure they be doing that right now. Sir William likes a cavalry patrol, he's a good horseman that knight of ours. But the plains be broad, they're four days hard ride to cross, and the same north to south. And that's a straight ride, no detours and no enemy to fight or keep a watch for. It be like a needle in a haystack. Not the King nor Sir William know where we are, nor where we might be coming out of the forest. We don't even know if Sir William is alive or not. We hope to see our cavalry patrols, aye, but just in case we'd best be depending on our own legs and brains for this trek home," replied Grim.

"Besides," added Herschel, "all the signs we've seen indicate that some of the wagons got through safely." He waved his hand towards the plains. "Somewhere ahead be our wagon train. And, I'd hazard to say, that His Majesty and Sir William trusts us two Bowmen to bring our visitors to safety. We're tough and be good at our craft, Grim 'n me." He finished with a proud grin.

"Yes, that be the truth, but right now we've got to get some food, we'll be mighty hungry by tonight. You say you are good at yer craft, what say we spend some time hunting and test yer skills?" suggested Clayton.

"Grim and me been watching for deer tracks. They be converging on a small pond nearby we know about. It be surrounded by sweet, thick grass not far ahead. We'll get there a'fore dark. We'll sit and wait for the animals to come in for a drink, then we'll have some meat for our dinner," smiled Herschel.

"Good," said Arthur. "I'm starved! I hope you Pentacles know how to cook as well as the cooks in the wagon train."

Eve and Natalie watched as Mondy carefully built a bark canoe. It looked unsteady and unwieldy, but they knew that they had few choices in transport other than walking.

Where Bowmen Grim and Herschel had led Follin's group east and then swung north towards the Swords Plains, Mondy took a safer path, but it was also the most difficult. They had only a single river to cross, the lower Pentacles River just before it branched into the Swords River and the River of Cups. The trek across the grassy plains, though, was the most dangerous. This was where most of the Wildlanders entered the forests to prey on the villages in the rich farmlands between the rivers.

"Ladies, this be necessary to take us down the river a few miles. It'll make it a little safer for us when we start our walk across the plains. Most of the Wildlanders enter the forests just north of here. So the further south we can get this canoe down towards the Swords River before it sinks, the better." Mondy shrugged his shoulders to ward off bad luck as he launched their canoe.

Holding the canoe steady he invited the two women to climb on board and sit down. It wobbled as he climbed in but remained afloat. Taking up a long, trimmed tree branch, he carefully steered the canoe into the middle of the Pentacles River.

"Ladies, please, don't move about too much, you'll tip us into the water. I hope that this canoe will stay afloat long enough to get us close to the Swords River, then we'll need to start walking again," said Mondy

Thus far, Mondy had proven to be an efficient and pleasant guide. He had proven that he was a proficient hunter over the past week of travel through the forest. They still had enough smoked venison for several more days if they rationed it.

Polling the canoe into the middle of the river he explained that he was hoping to land at a place he knew well. This, he explained was his old stomping grounds from childhood, but once they began their walk across the plains it would be much more dangerous.

They almost made it to the river junction when their canoe began to sink. Guiding it to a sandy bank, Mondy stood knee deep in the water as the two women climbed out.

"A day in that blasted contraption and I can barely walk. At least we have food enough for a few extra days." Now that Natalie knew Arthur was safe and not too badly injured she had begun to almost enjoy their adventure.

"Don't forget, to pick up your bag, Natalie. Mondy needs his hands free so that he can protect us delicate ladies of the court," reminded a giggling Eve.

By evening, Mondy had found a suitable low hill where he could set up their camp. "We'll camp here for a day or two. I'm quite certain that Sir William's cavalry will patrol this way looking for us," he said confidently. "This area beside the river is generally part of his patrol route. If we can see him it will be from up here. It's not too high to attract the attention of the Wildlanders but it's high enough to give us a good view of the surrounding plain. We'll make a dry fire to use as a smoke signal. If we see our cavalry out on the plain we can light it as a signal beacon."

The girls went to work collecting dry grass for their mattresses and their smoke signal while Mondy dug a shallow bed in the ground. It was just deep enough to stop the cold night wind from blowing on them as they slept. He then took some time to dig out a large pit for their fire to keep the flames below ground so as not to give their position away.

"Don't be afeared if you hear the wolves hereabouts," Mondy advised the girls. "They have been my village's companions for hundreds of years. They rarely venture into the forest, preferring the game on the plains. Whenever we go patrolling out here they always come to investigate and clean up our scraps after we've left."

Natalie wasn't so sure. "But what about the forest wolves? The Hilltown villagers were afraid of them, I heard them talking."

"Yes, the forest and mountain wolves are less tolerant of people," answered Mondy. The wind was picking up and he spoke softly so that his voice didn't travel with it. "We compete with them for food, so they don't like us too much. They don't come out to the plains very often, and if they do, they get chased away by the plains packs. They're strictly territorial and will fight to the death if they find a wolf from another pack on their land. I will say though, with some certainty, that we're quite safe here."

"What about the smell of the food we've cooked, or the smoke, won't that travel on the wind? If there are Wildlanders in the area they might smell it," said Eve.

Mondy was up to answering every one of the girl's questions which kept coming all afternoon and into the evening. "We cooked and ate early enough before the wind picked up. Tomorrow morning the wind will swing around to the east and we'll cook just on sunrise before it picks up and starts blowing our scent into the forest." He looked at the stars above, a mass of bright lights almost so bright it hurt to look at.

The night sky was a curtain of stars dropping right down to the horizon. "I think we need to turn in. We don't have much in the way of blankets so pull your grass bundles over as best you can. If it does get cold, we'll all snuggle up together for warmth."

With that comment, the girls looked at each other and started to giggle. Mondy was tall and handsome with an archer's powerful frame. The girls decided that a good looking young man was never difficult to snuggle up to. They wouldn't mind if it got cold, not one little bit.

The night was cold after all and the three snuggled up together for warmth. Bowmen were trained to manage all forms of discomfort on patrol, but three people in one bed-hole was torture for the polite young man. Monday was happily married to a lively young woman, and he knew to be on his best behaviour with royalty, so he kept his discomfort to himself.

Out in the forest and plains it was common for the men to sleep together because of the cold, especially when the winds from the north brought an early frost on their breath. On this occasion Mondy was left on the very edge with his back exposed to the wind. In the morning he woke with an aching back and an unhappy disposition.

"Good morning, Mondy. That was the best night's sleep I've had in a long time," announced Eve as she stretched her arms above her head.

"Lucky you then. I had the worst night sleep. I've got a chill in my back and I hardly slept because of the cold wind blowing down from the mountains," he said grumpily.

"Oh, I'm sorry." Eve stood and straightened her dress. "Give me a moment to splash my face and I'll see what I can do to help."

Hearing the two talking Natalie awoke and sat up.

"What?" she asked curiously. "What are you going to do with Mondy, Eve?"

"I'm going to fix the chill in his back that's what I'm going to do," Eve replied brightly.

"I've got to see this!" said Natalie as she climbed out of their sleeping-hole. She too stretched to ease the tension of sleeping in such an awkward position. "No matter how warm one can get, it's the cramping that's made my back sore as well," she hinted.

Eve knew what she was hinting at. "OK, I'll do some healing on you too."

When she was ready Eve, the healer, knelt on the ground and placed her hands on Mondy's back. She closed her eyes and tapped into the energy furnace at the centre of her being, just behind her navel. With three breaths she generated enough energy to move it into her hands and then into Mondy's aching muscles.

Within seconds a flood of warmth struck Mondy and he groaned in ecstasy.

"Oh, the lords on high have touched me," he groaned. "I can feel it, Eve, you've got a gift indeed. A little to the left... higher... higher... a bit more... ah, that's it, hold it there."

"My goodness, what are you doing girl?" squealed Natalie. "I want what he's having! Hurry up, Mondy, heal faster, it's my turn!" Natalie laughed out loud at the faces the young archer was pulling.

When Eve finished her healing, Mondy slowly straightened his back, his eyes opened and a broad smile of joy lit up his face. Eve was delighted at the results of her healing work.

"That was wonderful, Mistress Eve. I've never felt anything like that before. I feel fantastic," he sighed, looking at Eve like he had never seen a healer before.

"OK, Natalie, sit there, on the edge of the fire pit, close your eyes and relax. No laughing, I've not done healing for some time now, so you both are getting more than your fair share."

Natalie couldn't stop giggling which set Eve off. She was giggling so much she had to force herself to settle so that she could tap into her life-force again. As soon as her mind was still she felt a surge of energy pass from her hands into Natalie.

Natalie arched backwards from its force. "Oh, oh, Eve... this is marvellous! I've not had this much pleasure since... well... you know..." she started giggling and of course that led Eve to start giggling all over again.

"OK, that's enough, Natalie. I'm exhausted, now I need a break," Eve said getting ahold of herself. "It's time for me to have a splash in the stream while you two cook me some breakfast. And make my cup of tea just right - not too hot, not too cold." She enjoyed their looks of satisfaction. She knew that she could tell them to do anything and they would have gladly obeyed.

There was a shallow inlet of the river close to their campsite. As she leaned down to splash her face in the water she saw a set of footprints. At first, she thought they might be her own but then she noticed they were of a different style from the Pentacles and Swords shoes too.

'Oh no, we're in trouble,' she said to herself.

Slowly, carefully, Eve lifted her head to scan the ground and the plains surrounding their hill. There was no one in sight so she decided to chance heading back to the campsite.

"Pst! Mondy, there's footprints at the stream," she whispered as soon as she was close enough to the campsite to be heard.

Mondy and Natalie both looked up in surprise.

"Quick, come in here with us, stay low." Mondy took control of the situation and quickly scanned the horizon, his bow and quiver of arrows in hand.

"You saw footprints, not of Pentacles nor Swords, not yours neither? Were the prints of soft-soled moccasins?" he asked.

"Yes, I think they were. It was hard to tell in the mud but, yes... come to think of it, that's what they were," she replied.

"Ah ha, do you know who they belong to?" teased Mondy, a smile now creeping across his face. "That be the elves from hereabouts. We don't see them very often. I think that is what you saw, an elf footprint."

"They must be Wood Elves of the Daru clan. They live in the forests between the Swords River and River of Cups. Sometimes they will hunt on the grassy plains too," added Natalie knowingly.

"Elves?" sputtered Eve. Her hands went to her face and then danced nervously about in the air. "Are they dangerous? The ones on the Mystic Isle certainly are, and cruel. They cast all sorts of horrible magic at us when we go hunting for herbs. They hate people going into their forests, and will often kill any trespassers they find. We should stay well away from them," Eve advised.

"Oh, that's terrible, but ours are really quite friendly. We've got so much land that we can live in peace along-side each other, but we rarely see them," replied Mondy. "If they don't like you they'll just make themselves disappear."

"So is it safe to have them this close to us?" Eve asked. When she saw both Mondy and Natalie nod their heads she relaxed, but just a little.

Mondy sat quietly pondering while the girls sat chatting about the elves. Natalie was in her element, now she had something new to talk about.

Mondy suddenly stood. "Ladies, I'm going to examine those prints. Sometimes a friendly elf will leave a gift. We need to leave one in turn, it would be impolite not to. Do either of you have something we could leave as a gift?"

Natalie thought for a moment then unlatched the chain from around her neck. Attached to it was a golden brooch. Although it was small, it was beautiful. It was made of three strands of gold wire woven into an intricate pattern that made the eyes continually scan around the design to find its ending and beginning.

Page Natalie held the brooch in the palm of her hand.

"Here, this is something anyone would treasure. If it makes for us to be elf-wise in our time of need, then use this please."

Eve heard her comment and was curious. "Natalie, what does 'elf-wise' mean?" she asked.

"It means someone who is wise to the way of elves, a friend. Some people are accepted as equals by the elves, that makes them friends, elf-wise. A lot of our soldiers and forest dwellers are elf-wise," Natalie replied, proud to be the one to educate this Mystic Isle girl in the ways of elves.

"Page Natalie, this be most precious, thank you. I'm sure it will please the elves to receive this gift. You might become elf-wise yourself."

Mondy accepted the brooch and walked carefully to the stream bed. He found, not a yard from where Eve had seen the footprints, a parcel of cloth. It was the colour of the forest leaves, made of a lightweight material and large enough to cover their three bodies while sleeping. Delightedly Mondy placed the brooch exactly where the cloth was laid then returned with their prize.

"Look at this! That's an amazing piece of cloth, my hands feel warm just from touching it," exclaimed Natalie. Indeed, the wind had yet to pick up, but there was still a chill in the air.

The three spent the day laying low so that they didn't break the skyline, all the while watching for any sign of Sir William and his cavalry. By evening they had seen nothing and it bothered them.

"I'm worried," grunted Mondy as he prepared the fire for their evening meal. "We've struggled against the forest fire, the message from Eve that the Wildlanders and their mages are after us, and now we see no sign whatsoever of our patrols. Something has gone wrong, badly wrong."

Follin's Meditation – Eight of Swords

The eighth picture showed a young woman bound and blindfolded. Surrounding her were eight swords stuck into the ground as though to fence her in. She appeared to be standing in a swamp with water at her feet. As Follin stepped into the picture he politely asked her what she was doing in such a strange position.

"Did someone swap your brain for a mud pie? What do you think I'm doing, dolt!" she said freely slinging insults at her querent.

"I'm very sorry. I can see that you're bound and surrounded by sharp blades, but I truly am quite worried for you," he said.

"Can't you see? I'm surrounded by bad outcomes, everything is bad. I have nowhere to turn without exposing myself to more harm." The girl groaned and squirmed against her restraints. "I am in no position to speak my piece. That was what put me here, I was too hasty, I spoke rashly without thinking. I must wait, that's all I can do. The opportunity will arise, of that I'm certain, but right now I dare not do a thing."

"Does that means that if you speak out now you will cut yourself?" asked Follin seeking clarity as was his want more often these days.

"Not necessarily. I am bound by many things in this very politically correct Kingdom of Swords. We are bound by rules, codes of practice, ethics and red tape. There are so many rules that everyone just pays lip service to them. Oh, no, they never get caught but I always do. My current situation came about because I failed to exercise political correctness at my workplace. I insulted the office girl who flirts outrageously with the managers. Blast, I have such a big mouth. I said the wrong thing and now I seek serenity to accept judgement and whatever punishment my managers hand me."

The girl paused to wriggle into a more comfortable position. "I am bound by those who hold my destiny in their hands."

She continued so as to expand on her explanation. "I often say the wrong thing and get myself into trouble. Sometimes I wish it were my mouth that was bound and not my eyes."

The woman sighed, a deep heart-felt sigh of resignation. "I must do what I must do and that means I must suffer my stupidity and indignity in silence." The girl sighed once more and bowed her head in surrender.

"So that means sometimes you might be unjustly judged and punished?" Follin asked, probing gently.

"Exactly! If those who judge me only knew that the office girl gets whatever she wants by flirting, that is an injustice too. I just can't help but blurt out what's on my mind... Now go away, leave me be. Bound like this I seek to still my mind and placate my feelings of injustice and humiliation. I must find peace within so that I can accept my destiny." The girl straightened as best she could and returned to her passive waiting.

Follin contemplated the girl's plight for a moment but refrained from asking more questions.

'So, this might be a way for me to manage situations in which I have no control over. I am forever saying the wrong things too. I know how she feels, I got into so much trouble at school for that same problem. I always opened my mouth before I thought to engage my brain. She is smart to seek serenity within because she has no control over her judgement. Perhaps, when I am embarrassed for saying the wrong thing, I could contemplate serenity too.'

As Follin came back to consciousness he pulled out his notebook to record his meditation. But then a thought came to him. 'If I keep saying the wrong thing why don't I train myself to stop, think and then speak? It would certainly make my life a lot easier. I might explore how to do that in my meditations in the future.'

This was such a valuable insight, he thought as he hurriedly wrote his meditation in his notebook before rolling over and falling asleep.

Nine of Swords

Tormented by excessive worry; pressing external issues; unresolved issues of a personal nature; tortured to choose between two pathways when neither seems satisfactory; fearfulness; a positive resolution hidden behind a veil of uncertainty and anxiety.

The six Blue-beards stood by as Mage Armitar tried to walk his entrapment circle.

"Damn! Blast! This is going to take me forever! My feet, my bleeding feet!" he cried flinging his hands violently into the air. "When I get my hands on those fool Brown-caps I'll slice the skin off their feet, strip by bloody strip!" The mage cursed and swore at each painful step. None of the Blue-beards moved to help him, they deliberately ignored him.

Suddenly the mage grunted and stood up straight, his sore feet forgotten. The Blue-beard warriors blanched and immediately took up a defensive stance.

"Can't you ruffians do something to help me?" came the mages strangled cry. But once more, he straightened as another arrow thudded into his chest. The sound was loud and sickening as a third arrow struck, between the previous two, right in the centre of his foul chest. Mage Armitar collapsed to the ground, dead.

A loud voice called from the edge of the trees. The Blue-beards turned towards the voice, their weapons drawn and at the ready.

"Friends, 'tis Jordan and Peck, Brown-caps of the Hindamar highlands. We're here to give pay-back to this villainous spider who threatened to kill us. Don't take offence, lads, it is nothing to do with you. It be payback for his evil wrongs."

The explanation convinced the Blue-beards that they were not under attack, this was an act of vengeance against the mage alone by their Brown-caps brethren.

The two Brown-cap archers stepped from the screen of trees and into the clearing. Peck placed his foot on the mage's chest and pulled his two arrows free. He spat in the dust beside the mage to ward off the evil eye that it is said all mages release upon their death. Jordan did the same as he retrieved his arrow.

"Peace be to thy soul, Mage Armitar. You needn't come after us for revenge, we'll just as likely all die soon enough," stated Jordan to the mage's body on the ground.

Just then a strong wind roared towards them. It spun the leaves and branches above the dead mage into a whirling madness. The Hindamar Mountain warriors put up their hands to cover their faces as they were spattered by a foul, black ash which just as quickly disappeared. Where the mage had fallen there was now nothing but a puddle of blood.

"They always give me the willies when they do that," grunted Brandar. He turned to look at the two visitors and spoke. "It appears that you Brown-caps are in a spot of bother again."

"Well met, fire-friend," said Jordan as he waved for the rest of their band to join them.

"Brandar, we're sorry to put you and your friends in a position where you could be joining us in damnation, but this mage was in our way." Drevin directed his comment to his fellow clan leader, Brandar.

"You've given us a quandary, Drevin, you and your murderous band." There was no humour in the Blue-beard leader's voice. "If we go back to camp without Mage Armitar, we'll be accused of murdering him. If we go back without your heads, they'll think we be complicit in his killing. It be the same thing, it be on our heads to explain away that scoundrel's death."

"Brandar, I know that we have given you a quandary. We know that you should kill us all now, without mercy. But Mage Armitar had to go, he was the most evil of them all. He was going to kill us, as you know, and we weren't going to give him that satisfaction." Snowy spoke up clearly to show that their motives were pure and honourable.

The Blue-beards had yet to lower their weapons. The two archers of their band still had an arrow resting against their bowstring; the other warriors kept their hands on the hilts of their swords. This was not lost on the Brown-caps.

"Brandar, I have condemned you and your band," his hands spread out to include the rest of the Blue-beards. "And I've condemned your families and your villagers. I now set before you this quandary and seek your assistance in resolving it, together, the Hindamar Mountain way." He looked at the men on both sides then said, "As warriors of honour."

Brandar nodded and signalled for his men to relax as the two groups sat down to parley. Drevin had well known that there would be a reckoning. The signs he caught from Brandar weren't positive, nor was this lost on his archer band.

"I have a boy, he is to meet us here at the Big Rock. We expect him today or tomorrow. It be my wish that he be spared thy considerations." Jordan wanted to get his word in now before the parley started.

"I speak for my friend, Jordan. The boy's name is Londar, you met him when we spent time in your home, James." Snowy nodded to one of the Blue-beard archers squatting with them in the parlay circle. The man nodded in reply.

"Yes, I know the boy, a respectful young fellow." Having said his piece James settled back to listen, his fingers remained nervously fidgeting with his bow.

Drevin reiterated the same. "I want the boy kept out of this parley, what we have done this day has nothing to do with him." He held his gaze steady until Brandar nodded his acceptance.

"If James says the lad be honourable, and Jordan, Snowy and you too Drevin, speak of his non-participation in this wicked and treacherous act against a mage under my care, then I say he be spared." Brandar looked at his men and they all nodded in agreement. Any betrayal of this promise would mean the severest of punishments at the hand of their leader.

"Right, that now brings us back to our quandary, doesn't it, Drevin?" said Brandar slowly, carefully measuring each word.

Drevin nodded his head knowingly. "Yes," he said just as slowly, just as solemnly. "There be a reckoning."

Drevin paused to breathe deeply, calming his mind he began the parley as required by tradition. "Brandar, it be thy call, what shall be thy reckoning? Did ye want one-on-one or a general melee? It be thy decision since you be the aggrieved. Make thy call."

Brandar looked at Drevin then at his men as he deliberately pulled his sword from its scabbard. From his pack he took a cloth and a stone then began to clean and polish his weapon.

"I'd like to melee but that be a waste of good men. That villainous scab-backed mage does nay deserve their sacrifice. It be us clan leaders alone, just you and me, Drevin. You can choose weapons, though I see that you have already done so," replied Brandar. Drevin had also lifted his own sword from its scabbard to polish it free of marks, as befitted the solemnity of the occasion.

"Aye, let it be so, brother." Drevin peered at the sky. "It be midday soon, let's meditate until the sun sits overhead then shall we begin our reckoning."

"Aye, that be our way." Brandar sat with his back against Drevin's. They both crossed their legs and meditated to make peace with their gods and to prepare for their soul's journey to the land of shadows. Each of the warriors knew that only one seated in the centre of the sacred circle would see the sunset this day.

The two groups silently completed the circle, already half drawn by the mage. It held no power as Mage Armitar had failed to complete his spell. It would now serve as an arena for the silent meditators at its centre.

Their colleagues solemnly cleared the space free of twigs, leaves and anything that might cause a man to slip or trip. Once that was completed, the men took food from their packs and built a communal fire. As part of the ritual performed before a blood reckoning, they cooked their leaders a last meal.

At exact midday Brandar and Drevin ended their meditations and joined their friends in their meal. The two ate sparingly, silently. They were aware that this would be the last meal for one of them.

At the completion of their meal, the men seated on the outer circle began to chant the mountain clan's traditional death song. It rose in pitch to suddenly cease, only to be taken up by a solitary voice, a lone singer. It was then joined in harmony by another voice from the other side of the circle. The two continued to sing, a song of the joys and discoveries of childhood; the romance and passions of adolescence; and finally, the pleasures of a family and participating in the communion of their people.

As the song ended the two leaders scanned the faces of their friends for the last time. Calmly they stood, their swords drawn as they faced each other from opposing halves of the circle.

The four Brown-caps sat silently lost in their own thoughts. Drevin smiled warmly at each of his friends in turn, they nodded but were unable to return his smile.

Drevin spoke as was his right as the initiator of the parley.

"I, Drevin, of the Hindamar Mountain highlands, beyond the Pentacles Kingdom; warrior, war leader of the Brown-caps, husband, son, friend and father, go to meet my destiny this day. I go without fear, to do honour to my people and my cause. I sought justice for the wrongs done to me and my villagers." He paused before continuing. "As the appointed mage of our village, Mage Armitar preyed upon and stole the youthful joy of union between husband and wife. It is to my shame that Mage Armitar raped my wife on our wedding night and I was powerless to prevent it. He hid the sun to leave our people in the darkness of sorrow. This day he planned to kill myself and my band, for nothing! Mage Armitar deserved to die and I am but sorry it wasn't at my hand."

Drevin saluted his men then turned to face his foe, his breathing was slow and deliberate. His face showed no emotion as his gaze fixated on something beyond the circle, perhaps it was something that only he could see.

"I, Brandar, warrior, proud war leader of the Blue-beards, of the eastern lowlands of the Hindamar Mountains bordering the Wands and Swords Kingdoms; husband, son, friend, father and killer of my people's enemies. My honour and the lives of my band, our families and villagers, have been threatened by the murder of a mage under my care and protection. I have only one course of action that will save my people, my family and my soul. Today I face my destiny and I be the hand of that destiny." He stopped for a moment to look at Drevin on the other side of the circle and he nodded in understanding. "I too am sorry, my friend, that Mage Armitar did not die by my own blade." Brandar stopped speaking, his head was bowed as he spoke this last sentence, a deep sadness wrestled across his face.

No one spoke nor moved. The two combatants stood as if carved in stone, neither wished to initiate what was to end in his fire-friend's death.

The silence was broken by Brandar's grunt as he hefted his sword and swung it in an arc above his head. He roared his clan's war cry as he stepped across the few yards of cleared ground to bring the blade down towards Drevin's body.

The Brown-cap leader didn't moved, he stood tall and proud, ready to accept his fate as the blade sliced through the junction of his neck and shoulder to bury itself deep in his chest. Brandar suddenly emerged from his trance and flinched in confusion. In shock he realised the enormity of what he had done.

It was over, honour had been satisfied and the Blue-beard's families would be safe. The two groups, most openly crying, prepared to go their separate ways.

The band of Brown-caps had known their leader would fight that day. They weren't afraid he would lose, Drevin's reputation with both bow and sword was legendary. What they failed to recognise was the depth and strength of his honour.

Peck looked at his friends for a moment, then, through his tears he spoke, "Lads, Drevin be the best of us. He would not be judged to have broken the sacred bond of fire-friend. There be none more honourable than he. So be his end. I shall never forget nor shall I allow our children and grand-children to forget."

Brandar had remained frozen above Drevin's body as Snowy and Jordan moved to prepare their leader for burial.

"Why didn't you fight? Why, Drevin, why?" Brandar asked as his body began to shake with emotion. "Drevin, my fire-friend, but you were more than that. We spent our youth training together, we romanced the girls together, we hunted together, we fought together... yet ye never told me of the evil which Mage Armitar did to thy wife..."

The proud leader of the Blue-beards, began to sob. "I'm sorry my friend, I never knew..." He drew a deep breath as he announced to both Wildlander bands. "Drevin was my friend and will remain in my heart to the day I die." The Blue-beard war leader now broke into gut-wrenching sobs. His powerful body shook as he dropped his sword and collapsed to his knees to bury his face in the bloodied chest of his friend.

"Aye, he be the best," said Snowy softly, his own tear streaked face creased with sorrow.

As they were singing the burial dirge over Drevin's grave, Londar ran into the clearing. He looked around counting only the four archers, Drevin was not there.

He was about to question his comrades when he remembered to show his respect - they were singing the Hindamar highlands dirge for the dead. At that moment Londar realised that their leader was the focus of the burial. He joined the others in their clan's death song, a song they had sung many a time this side of the Hindamar Mountains. His hands began to shake and tears dripped from his eyes as he felt the depth of sadness around him. He had no idea what had happened, but he wouldn't interrupt the solemnity of this moment, not for anything.

The following day Follin's band continued their trek between the rivers with full bellies from a young deer the archers had taken. They finally crossed the Swords River and set up camp just before nightfall. It was a valiant effort for the band to travel as far as they had in those few days, but now they were exhausted and needed to rest.

Sitting on the ground waiting for his meal Arthur decided to ask Frailbones how he did *that light energy breathing thing*.

"Aye, I can show thee now we have a few hours 'afore bed. But first let me see to thy arm, it's moving about like it's alive. I don't think it's broken, perhaps it has a wee crack in it. Maybe the mage who dressed it knew how to heal. He would have done for your arm what I showed you earlier and what caused me to slow everyone down from fatigue."

Frailbones closed his eyes as he placed his hands on Arthur's arm. Follin watched carefully trying to sense what the old man was doing so that he too could learn how to do it.

"Aye, it's healing nicely. I think we'll run through that exercise now." He directed Arthur to lie down and close his eyes but was immediately interrupted by Follin's questions.

"Sorry to interfere, Frailbones, but what did you just do? I think it was what I do to sense the forest wisdom, but somehow it's different. Can you please teach me too?" he asked, his eyes bright with anticipation.

"Aye, lad, that I can do." Frailbones indicated for Follin to lie on his back beside Arthur. As they settled he began to instruct them in the healing arts that he had learned more than half a century earlier.

As Frailbones set about teaching his healing meditation, the two Pentacles men-at-arms set up camp in their usual efficient and orderly manner. They next prepared the fire to cook more of their venison and some root vegetables gathered on their trek. When the two Bowmen arrived back from scouting the area around their campsite, they commented on the work of the Pentacles soldiers.

"Look 'ere Private Grim, Pentacles lads have built us a wee house inside the ground, they have," joked Herschel indicating the admirable workmanship of the fire-pit.

"My my, Private Herschel, 'tis the work of the God Vulcan himself," answered Grim joining in the fun. "Look, I sit on the side and I can touch the ground with me feet. I can reach across to yon fire and slice meself a piece of venison. This be the work of a master Pentacles crafter indeed."

"Silly beggars," grunted Clayton wiping the tears from his eyes as a thin stream of smoke swirled around him. "You lads have never seen a fire-pit like this have ye. Corp and I are both Hindamar Mountain born and bred, we knows how to make a fire-pit that hides the flames but gives off a particularly nice warmth all through the night. We spent our time with the Mountaineers we did, before signing on to run patrols with the wagon trains to help you lazy sods out."

"Aye, 'tis the work of masters, we give thee that, Private Clayton." Herschel said sitting beside his mate, Grim, and warming his hands by the cosy fire.

The pit was simply a circular trench carved into the ground big enough to fit a half-dozen men. While the seating platform was below ground level to keep those seated out of the wind, the fire was set on a lower earthen platform in the middle. It was perfect to hide the light of their fire while keeping the occupants warm.

"I bet we lads can sleep in 'ere too," teased Grim as he unslung his quiver of arrows and set it behind him away from the heat of the fire.

As the men chatted among themselves, Frailbones continued to teach the youths their meditation. He had become a little more animated once they'd passed the River of Cups.

Follin wasn't quite sure what was going on with his old Pentacles friend, but by Sox's actions, sticking close to Frailbones all that day, he was fearful of what it could be. He sensed that Frailbones was unwell but he was unsure as to its cause.

"Now close yer eyes lads and put yer mind in yer navel. Breathe as though that be yer nose. Think of a warm bright light going in and out of yer navel just like it were air. Imagine that thy lungs be in yer belly and thy nose be thy navel. Can ye feel the tickle of the air going in and out?" He continued for the next thirty minutes, guiding the boys to breathe light energy into their navel centre and to fill their belly with a healing warmth that they could then channel to any part of their body. Follin knew this meditation from his time with The Empress, but it was Frailbones novel manner of instruction that captivated him.

At the end of their meditation the group gathered in the fire pit for their meal. Arthur spoke softly for the night was dark and no one knew what might be lurking in the darkness beyond.

"Hey, Follin, our master wagoneer is also a master healer," whispered Arthur leaning forward to slice off a piece of venison on the spit above the fire. "I never knew people could do things like that. Isn't it amazing what one can learn from a humble wagoneer?" he chuckled and dug Frailbones in the ribs playfully.

"Hey, Page Arthur, where did ye get all that energy? Last I saw you was collapsed on the ground after running all day," called Corporal Owens in a soft voice, he too was in a jovial mood.

"Well, Corporal Owens," said Arthur just as lightly. "I don't rightly know. I was exhausted and I couldn't take another step, but now here I am ready to run another day."

As the men chatted and joked, Follin and Frailbones moved aside to talk of healing, meditation, energy transfer and of how to sense someone's energy and to meld with their patient.

"I know about melding, Frailbones, but what you did was different. I can meld with trees but melding with a person is new to me," declared Follin.

"Nothing to it, lad. Close yer eyes again and I'll put my hand on thy arm and send my mind into your body. I want you to follow what I do."

"Yes, I'll follow you," answered Follin eagerly.

Frailbones placed his hand on Follin's bare arm and sent his mind into the youth's body. All the while he could sense Follin's awareness of his actions.

There was a moment when Follin's mind wandered and he remembered what the King and Queen of Swords had said about honour. He recalled how he should apologise to Frailbones for dishonouring him when Londar was with them.

In this state of vulnerability Follin shuddered and came back to consciousness - he had broken out in a cold sweat. The Mystic Isle youth was momentarily confused, dazed and agitated. As he tried to speak he began to stutter, then he had to lie back down to stop the world spinning.

"It's all right lad. I used a tad too much energy, that's all. I went very deep into thy body. I must say though, that yer health is perfect." Frailbones didn't know what the problem was but he was nonetheless worried at Follin's reaction.

"I've got to talk to you, Frailbones, that's what this is about. I failed to apologise for disregarding your honour when I talked Londar into staying with us and thus putting his life at risk. The King and Queen of Swords suggested that I make amends for disrespecting your promise to Londar's father, Jordan. I'm sorry, it was wrong of me." Follin confessed. Suddenly he felt as though a heavy burden had been lifted from his shoulders. This was an unexpected reaction, he thought.

"Lad, I forgave thee the moment you did it. I knew what thy intention was, it was to save Arthur and myself. It took me a minute to work it out. I'm getting a tad slow in my old age."

"I should have considered your situation and I failed to do that." Follin looked at his aged friend in relief.

"Follin, you be thinking of our safety, and Londar gave his consent. I knew you were trapped. It was a case of carrying the two of us, or to leave us while you went to get help. In both cases, young Page lad and I would have perished in the fire. Instead lady luck whispered in your ear and thee followed her instructions. Here we be today, alive and having the time of our lives. I can live with my pride being bruised, so can thee.

Here, shake on it." The old man extended his gnarled hand, the two shook hands as true friends should.

"Now we're at peace with ourselves and the world. Let's grab some of that sweet-smelling venison before the lads eat it all."

It was about then that there came a sharp 'Click!' 'Click!' from the darkness beyond the firelight. It was a Bowman signal seeking permission to enter their camp. Immediately the group grabbed their weapons and melted into the darkness.

"Permission to join you good men at your meal," stated a firm but pleasant voice.

Follin's ear's pricked up.

"Hey, I know this man, it's Sir Darwyn, the Charioteer," called Follin softly.

Corporal Owens spoke firmly into the darkness, "Stranger, walk this way and be known to us."

Into the dim firelight walked a tall, dark-haired man. He wore a sword at his waist and his armour was pitted and scored with the marks of many battles.

"I heard you chatting and I could smell your meal roasting. I am Sir Darwyn, and I would be obliged for your hospitality, kind sirs," announced the Charioteer nodding in recognition to Follin.

"Welcome to our camp, Sir Darwyn. If you be Follin's friend then you be ours." The Pentacles Corporal invited the warrior to sit with them and share their meal.

"Thank you, but I also have a shy friend. He is waiting just beyond the firelight. May I invite him to join us?" The Charioteer saw the look of distrust race around the soldiers' faces. It was not the warrior's code to leave uninvited guests in the dark, not when their hosts were back-lit by their campfire, vulnerable and eating their meal.

"Sir Darwyn, 'tis poor form to leave a man waiting in the dark while he himself be filling his belly. Bring yon friend in and any others ye have hidden in the darkness." Grim rested his hand on the knife at his waist, they all felt somewhat vulnerable, aggrieved and uncomfortable.

Sir Darwyn whistled lightly. Out of the darkness stepped a slim, handsome man. He had fair features, brown hair and clothed in the colour of the forest glen. In his hands he carried a bow and on his back was a quiver of arrows. A thin bladed knife was sheathed at his back.

"Welcome, fair elf of the woods," Herschel greeted the visitor. "'Tis uncommon for your kind to drop in on the guardsmen of the Kingdom. Please sit and partake of our sparse meal."

The elf stepped into the fire-pit to reach the venison roasting on its spit and sliced himself a piece of meat. He nodded in recognition to Frailbones first, then to the Bowmen, before sitting between Sir Darwyn and Arthur - to Arthur's absolute delight.

"This beast on thy fire-spit, he be the wee buck, Two Spots," came the elf's respectful, softly spoken voice. "We had planned to take him for our meal in another year when he was older. We wished to give him time to enjoy the sunshine, play with his friends and to enjoy the sweet grasses next spring. Alas, his time came earlier than anticipated. But his gift of life is not wasted." The elf sat comfortably on the edge of the pit and started eating.

"I suppose you would like an explanation of why Ziggy and myself are here?" asked Sir Darwyn as he sliced another piece of meat from the spit.

Follin had found his tongue and answered. "We would love to hear that, but, Sir Darwyn, where is your chariot?"

"My chariot is in the Pentacles Kingdom for repairs, Follin," he chuckled as though it was a joke. "Lads, these are wild times, are they not? I bring some good news – boys, your wives are fine. In fact, they are not too far away, north and west of here. They are, like us, in some danger, surrounded by Wildlander patrols. I've come to lend you all a hand. Ziggy's clan is keeping an eye on the girls for you. He's agreed to guide you to them."

The group turned to look at each other. Arthur broke the stunned silence.

"Are the girls harmed?" he asked anxiously.

"Arthur, they're fine, no harm will come to them. Ziggy's people have them hidden and have been protecting them all this time. But the Wildlander mages are searching for the two Mystic Islanders. They're far from happy to have let you, Follin, and your wife, slip through their fingers," replied Sir Darwyn.

Ziggy spoke once more, his voice soft but clear.

"We'll eat while we can, then you need to collect your weapons and gear then we'll be off. It will take us all tonight and much of tomorrow. We travel safely, for the most part, but the closer we get to our destination the more danger we are in." With a grin he added, "Now don't forget my mug of tea, Grim, I have taken quite a liking to your Swords brew. Herschel, elf-wise, put the billy on again and let's relax for a while before we have to leave." His legs swung back and forth as he kicked his heels against the fire pit's dirt walls in anticipation.

"Follin, did you get that? Eve and Natalie are safe. The Wood Elves have been protecting them, we'll see them at last. I can't wait!" Arthur exclaimed with relief.

"Lad," said the elf, "your archer friend, Mondy, has been their champion through the forest and onto the plains. He's elf-wise, as are Herschel and Grim here. Mondy has been the hero, not us. We've just kept an eye out for them, that's all."

"Mondy's a local, he knows these parts like the back of his hand," said Herschel in a rare display of animation. "Your wives be in safe hands with Mondy, have no fear of that, lads."

The next morning saw the troop of Brown-cap archers jogging their way towards the Hindamar Mountain ranges. They had spent the night standing vigil at their war leader's grave. At the rising of the sun they said their farewells and set out for home. They each knew that the moment the mages heard of their treachery, the men's families and their village friends, would be forfeit.

"Jeb, you lead and set the pace, you've got young eyes. Jordan, you and Londar take the rear. No matter what happens one of us must make it home to warn our people. If the mages get there first then our efforts are wasted." Snowy, the eldest of the band, had taken command to lead the archers home.

There was a low mist lying just above ground level. It helped hide the Brown-caps, but not for long. From atop their horses the cavalry scouts spotted the archers running across the plains just as the mist began to lift.

"Captain Sheckle, it's a small band of Brown-caps running north," called one of the horsemen.

"Right, lads, form up left and right wings, we'll ride them down. These Wildlanders will never learn will they?" Captain Sheckle led one of several cavalry squadrons patrolling the Swords Plains.

The squadron, sixty horse strong, now raced across the grass-covered plain to intercept and run down the archer band.

The Brown-cap's first warning was the rumbling of horses hooves on the ground. Snowy called the command to scatter. He knew from the thundering sound of so many horsemen that this was going to be his last fight.

"Boy, stay by me, we fight this battle together," called Jordan, his breath rasping in his throat.

No archer likes a cavalry charge. The archers were as vulnerable as any could be - running on the open plains, pursued by horsemen with lances and swords. They knew, in their hearts, that this would be their end, and each would soon join their war leader, Drevin.

"One of us must get back to the village!" cried Snowy only seconds before he was pierced by a Swords lance.

Jeb managed to fire three arrows in rapid succession before he too was knocked to the ground. Jordan and Londar turned when they heard Snowy cry out. They stood together, father and son, each nocked an arrow to their bows and released it at their foe. They had no time for a second volley before Jordan was run through and his son, Londar, knocked to the ground by the rearing war-horse.

"All clear, Captain Sheckle," said one of the cavalry troopers. "It's just a small band. They've probably had enough of fighting and wanted to get home to their wives and children."

"Don't we all," sighed Captain Sheckle. He turned in his saddle to yell at his troop. "Collect their weapons and let's get back to patrolling." He paused a moment, noticing the youth lying on the ground. The boy moved his arm and tried to stand up.

"Lad here is wounded, pick him up and we'll take him back with us. I've had a gut-full of killing. When he's healed we can send him home."

Cavalry Sergeant Poppinjoy dismounted and stepped over to the boy. "Lad, stay down, let me look you over." He stopped Londar from sitting up then checked him for wounds. "Yer fine, that head knock doesn't look too bad."

Londar started to stand, shaken and confused. It had happened so fast that he was unsure where he was or what had happened. Then he saw his father lying beside him, pierced by a lance.

"Da!" he screamed and threw himself onto his father's chest. "NO! Da! No, no, no! Don't die, nooo..." His hysterical sobbing was muffled by his face thrust into his father's chest.

The sergeant waited, he'd seen this before and had felt those same feelings of loss and grief, many times. *'Best let the lad cry it out now, lest he has regrets later,'* he reminded himself.

After a time Sergeant Poppinjoy bent down and pulled Londar upright. He brushed the boy's limp body free of dirt and leaves. Then, noticing Londar's weapons lying on the ground he picked them up. He saw the boy's eyes staring at his father's weapons and so his gathered these as well. Leaning down Poppinjoy respectfully covered the man's face with his torn jacket sleeve, then handed Londar and Jordan's bows, quivers and knives to one of his troop.

"Corporal Travers, organise a party to dig the graves, we'll give them a proper burial." Turning to Londar, he said, "Lad, take the shovel and help. That be thy father? Yes? Then it be your duty to bury him. These be your friends and uncles?" Again Londar nodded woodenly. "Then we'll not leave until they be buried proper. Now I want you to do your duty to your family. We'll help you to do the right thing and honour them with you."

The party were finished by midday and caught up with Sir William and the remaining wagons soon after. Sergeant Poppinjoy wanted to make sure the young Brown-cap was safely tended to and no harm came to him. There was just something good and pure about the boy and he wanted to make sure it wasn't bashed out of him by the stupidity and insensitivity of warfare.

No one had noticed the lone figure stand to silently blend with the melting mist. The Brown-caps archer soon began to jog towards the far Hindamar Mountains. Peck, the band's lone survivor, was intent on surviving the hostile Swords Plains and the freezing mountain ranges. His message was vital to the survival of his family and that of his friends and villagers.

Follin's Meditation – Nine of Swords

Follin was restless, he couldn't fall asleep. He kept tossing and turning as thoughts of the troubles faced by Eve and his friends flooded his mind. He deliberately put his worries aside to focus on the image in one of the pictures Page Natalie had handed him. It showed a man sitting up in bed with his face in his hands. By his bed were nine swords arranged in line on the wall.

'I don't want to go in there. This image is all about anguish and I certainly don't need to revisit that,' Follin thought.

As he contemplated the image Follin had to face the fact that this was another vital lesson on his Swords journey that could not be put off.

'I'll make sure to seek clarity because that is the Swords objective.'

"Sir," he said softly, "what bothers you so much that it makes you sit up in your bed tonight in such obvious distress?"

"I'm grieving the foolishness of my life. I've made mistakes and I've missed opportunities. I should have avoided action in some situations, and acted in others but failed to do so."

"What is the lesson you have learned from your misfortune, sir?" Follin wanted to get this meditation over with as quickly as possible while being sensitive to the poor man's suffering.

"Lad, my anguish seeks to show you one of the main barriers to a clear mind. The Swords lessons are all directed at learning how to use your mind to its fullest potential. In this journey through my kingdom you have been shown how to recognise denial; to place emotion and feeling aside; to see through irrational explanations; to confront denial; and to use the powers of observation to find the clear definition of an issue or dilemma. My anguish illustrates a special lesson for you: fail to manage your mind's wilfulness and you may end up tormenting yourself when you should be sleeping."

Follin reflected for a moment then asked, "Sir, I lie awake at night and worry over things I can't control. I worry about Eve and my friends who *have been sent to attack the Wildlander's fort; Frailbones and Londar, Arthur and Natalie... no wonder I'm struggling to fall asleep tonight. Are these the sorts of things that worry you as well?"*

"Lad, we have a saying in our kingdom that one should cultivate internal calm to manage those issues that we cannot control; the strength of character to deal with the things that we can control; and the clarity and wisdom to understand the difference between the two," replied the man now leaning on his elbow studying Follin.

"Thank you, sir. I shall do my best with this lesson which has presented many times in my meditations." Follin felt a warm glow inside as he was at last beginning to grasp the lessons of the Swords Kingdom.

"Lad, clarity of meaning allows you to harness the power of your mind but this must be done in conjunction with other mental practices. These include ignoring ill-informed or overly emotional opinions; making wise choices; waiting patiently and strategically for the right moment to act; and recognising that which is beyond your power to control and that which is. Practice them all and you will touch upon the lessons of the Swords."

Ten of Swords

Hitting rock-bottom; it can't get any worse; giving in to the universe is the only option; the end of an arduous and painful episode.

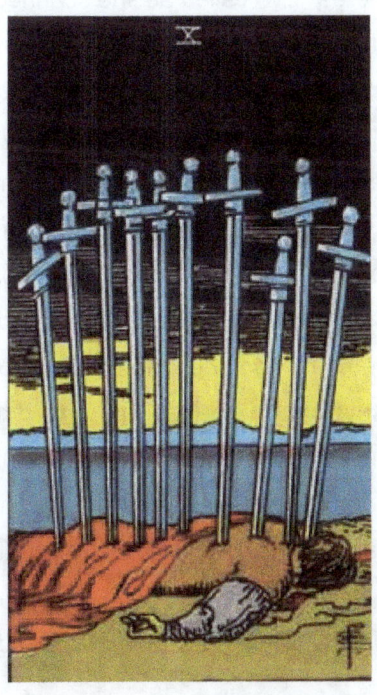

Eve woke at false dawn, there was still plenty of time for her to stay in comfort under the warm elven blanket. As awareness came to her she could feel the radiant warmth from Mondy and she could hear Natalie's light breathing, both were still sound asleep. She felt safe and secure knowing the Wood Elves were protecting them.

'*How strange to be guarded by friendly elves,*' she thought, recalling the many horror stories she had heard of her Mystic Isle elven clans.

The elven coverlet really did feel enchanted. She could barely feel its weight yet it shed a warmth that kept out the cold and enlivened her spirit. Woven into its cloth Eve sensed themes of sleep, warmth and contentedness much like a mother's lullaby. She giggled silently at that thought, fancy the elves thinking humans were children.

Restless and now fully awake, she decided to visit Molly and see how she was faring.

"Molly, are you there?" Eve called as she scanned with her third eye around their campsite. Instead of grassland and bushes, what she saw was quite different to what she expected. Surrounding their camp was a mist, an impenetrable gloom that the eye shied away from.

'That must be the Wood Elves' doing,' she thought absently.

'It certainly is, Mistress Eve,' came Molly's voice inside her head. *'Please, arise, I wish to introduce you to my friends of the Daru Clan.'*

Suddenly Eve came back from her meditation and felt an urge to go to the same inlet where she had seen the elven footprint. On arriving at the inlet she saw a small group of elves who invited her to sit with them.

"We created the mist that you see around your camp to stop the Wildlander mages from sensing you. They're watching, right now they're free-floating in the astral plane trying to pick up your trace," said an older, matronly elf.

"What about Follin, can they find him?" Eve asked, her voice soft but tense with worry.

"He has his own magic, Eve. Follin doesn't even know it but his body wisdom sometimes shuts out inquisitive minds. But all-the-same we've sent Ziggy to bring him here with his friends. Ziggy will make sure they remain unseen," came the elven woman's reply.

"Did you say he's coming here?" Eve was excited but she was also troubled. What if something happens on their trip? Mondy did say that the Wildlanders were all around, that's why they had to stay low and out of sight.

"My dear, all is fine. It is safe here."

"But why didn't you contact us when we started? That would have made it so much easier," asked Eve.

This time one of the males answered. Three wicked claw marks across his face lent a fierceness to his intense gaze. At his crossed feet lay a bow and quiver of arrows.

"Eve, if we had let you know earlier, you would have let out a psychic beacon that would have drawn every mage in the land. We did it in a safer manner, a blanket for a brooch, nothing too obvious. '*Just keep it simple*' is our motto with humans." His grin had the effect of softening his appearance. "Humans, not all but most, aren't the smartest of creatures in the land."

Eve blushed, she certainly agreed.

"So, what do we do next? We've got to get to the Swords castle, we've lost a lot of our friends and our training has gone to rack-and-ruin."

Molly's voice soothed the panic building within Eve's mind. "*Eve, this journey is your training. Sometimes we have to take our lessons as the opportunity presents. You have been fortunate, however, you have powerful allies. Each has taken pains to protect and guide you. So rest assured that you have not wasted a single day of your lessons, the whole world is your classroom.*"

"Eve," continued the matronly elf, "when Ziggy arrives with your husband our mission will be complete. We need to get back to protecting our forests and plains. We may meet again, if destiny wills it. Now tell your friends that you spoke to us and for them to stay within the sanctuary that we have built for your safety."

―――

The night air had grown bitterly cold by the time they set out to meet with Eve, Natalie and Mondy. Follin's band however felt uplifted by Sir Darwyn and the elf's presence. The Charioteer did not stop talking for most of the evening. He remained up front with the four soldiers where they shared their stories of adventure and battles of old. To the four warriors this would be a night they would never forget. It was one to tell at every campfire and tavern they visited. Ziggy stayed with the others.

Follin noticed how the elf paid particular attention to Frailbones. He sensed that his elvish presence may have triggered memories sometimes best left in the past. Ziggy, too, sensed the fluctuations in the old man's mood, it was a sign he'd seen in humans of great age before. He stayed close to help if and when it might be needed.

As they walked they swapped stories of their own. Frailbones demonstrated an encyclopedic knowledge of elven lore. Both Follin and Arthur were amazed at the breadth and depth of their modest wagoneer's experiences.

"How on earth do you know all that, Frailbones? I can't believe that anyone would know so much about elves and magic," whispered Arthur, his face showed admiration and amazement on so many occasions that Follin had to remind him to close his mouth, otherwise his jaw would drag on the ground.

"Lads, I've lived and learned, that's all. Maybe old Ziggy here might tell you some stories of his own instead of listening to my boring old memories," replied the wagoneer with a tired smile.

"This old man forgets that he has been elf-wise for longer than most humans alive today. He has lived way beyond the age when most humans have passed to the shadowlands," Ziggy explained. Frailbones nodded slowly in agreement. "Perhaps he will tell you a little of how he rescued one of our kind many years ago."

The two youths were now completely hooked. Arthur was once more open-mouthed and desperate to know the story.

"What happened?" he asked.

"Now that is up to speculation, he's never told anyone. It is said that he slew an evil mage with his sword during the rescue. Why don't you tell the young men the story, my friend?" suggested the elf.

Old Frailbones was happy, as happy as he could remember, being with his old friend Ziggy made him feel complete. He knew that this was an illusion, for out beyond the elf's screen of invisibility lay those who wished to kill them. The old man had another reason to feel happy, a lifelong burden was soon to be lifted from his shoulders.

"Lads, 'twas a very long time ago and yet I still feel the pain of loss. This story has a beginning and an ending. My telling it to ye tonight be its ending. It completes a promise I made that I have put off for way too long. Tonight it be time to tell the 'story never told'."

While the band walked softly through the night Frailbones spoke clearly wanting to give his story a proper voice.

"I had just entered manhood as a journeyman Wagoneer, fully twenty-one years of age. Living those twenty-one summers and winters in the Pentacles Kingdom had filled me with a curiosity and a burning desire to know more about the world. I left my home to find work with the Hindamar Mountain highlanders, those we call the Brown-caps. I'd visited them several times during my wagoneering apprenticeship so I knew them quite well. After a year or so I left the highlands to explore the rest of our Tarot Empire. My adventures began when I was captured by a band of Wildlander swordsmen returning to their homes. They had been fighting for some months in the Wands Kingdom. When they learned that I knew the Brown-cap archer's secret signs they let me go.

"It was while travelling in the hills bordering the Swords Plains a few weeks later that I learned of an elf-lass held prisoner by Wildlander mages. The head mage was but a youth at that time, 'twas the evil Mage Armitar, that same one we met with Londar's band, the one who tried to take you away from us, Arthur." He paused as Arthur nodded slowly remembering the story of his capture and rescue.

"After hearing of the villainous mages reputation from my highland friends I knew that this poor elf-lass was in grave danger. What better adventure could a young man have than to rescue a beautiful elf-lass? Her name was 'Naroo the Pretty'. With a name like that I had no choice but to try and rescue her. My friends knew of this mage, they spoke of him in hushed tones for fear he would know of their thoughts. He was much younger then, cruel, mean and vicious. He tortured his own people, the villagers that he was sworn to protect. I'll speak no more of that scoundrel. Just know that he deserves what he gets and I hope one day it is a knife in his black heart."

"Frailbones," Ziggy placed a hand on his friend's arm, "it is almost dawn, we need to make camp. Would you please honour us and continue with your story as we eat?"

The group stopped on a low rise in the plains. They could see for miles but there were no Wildlander or Swords patrols in sight. Again the Pentacles soldiers dug a hole big enough for everyone to sit within, a fire burned brightly at its centre. They carefully warmed their left over venison and a stew of beans and vegetables, a delicious elven dish Ziggy had brought with him. As they sat back, satiated and warmed by the fire in the chill of the predawn air, the boys asked Frailbones to continue his story.

"What story is that Frailbones? I must have missed the start of it. I think you've more stories of adventure than I have," announced Sir Darwyn.

"It is the 'story never told', of how he rescued the elf-girl, Naroo the Pretty," answered Follin.

At hearing the girl's name from another's lips, Ziggy hung his head and let out a sigh that made Follin look closely at him.

"I haven't heard that story either. No one knows the truth of the 'story never told' but Frailbones himself." Sir Darwyn said as he settled himself on the floor of the fire-pit and pulled a pouch of tobacco from his shirt. He filled his pipe then offered the tobacco to the others. The soldiers reached for the pouch in delight and packed their clay-pipes in turn. Slowly the air began to smell of the sweet, aromatic scents of the forests.

Frailbones was not going to be rushed. He waited in turn to pack his own smoke-blackened pipe, then sat with his back against the warm fire-pit wall.

"Aye, 'tis a story that is ready to be told, I'll grant thee that. The pain that be from my memories has since passed, at least enough to tell the tale. I can now speak of it without shedding tears of wrath and sadness. But in the telling and in the listening, I warn you all, there be a price that must be paid."

The band were a little confused by his warning but soon shrugged it off as an old man's way with words. They now waited, watching as Frailbones drew deeply on his pipe, then he began.

"As I was telling these lads, I was young, full of piss 'n wind. I was seeking an adventure so that I could tell stories like this in my old age." He chuckled, his head down, remembering, a few tears began to slide down his weathered cheek.

"The Wildlanders spoke of a beautiful elf-lass held prisoner by their mages on the plains of the Swords Kingdom. I asked around to discover exactly where she might be. She was a Wood Elf of the Daru Clan, sister to Ziggy and Kerrytan. Ziggy knows more than he lets on, but he has his own grief to deal with so I will nay say more on that. This was during the early days of the Wildlander invasions. A rogue band of mages had sent their spies into the Tarot Kingdom and found the sweet elf-lass Naroo and captured her."

"How did they find her? I thought elves were magical and could'na be caught," announced Clayton blowing a thin stream of smoke from between his lips.

"Lass had been attacked by a wolf, one of the mage's dogs. It was nay the wolf's fault, it be doing what it was told. It brought the elf-lass to the mages camp in its jaws and they decided to have some fun with her before they killed her."

"How come she did'na escape with her magic, then?" again Clayton was quick to ask before Frailbones could continue.

"Clayton," answered Ziggy softly. "If you capture an elf and bind them with magic they can't escape. They can't even contact their family and friends for help. My sweet sister Naroo was a prisoner and completely at the mercy of the mages. Now let the old man tell his story will you."

"It's all right, Ziggy, lad knows naught of elven ways. I don't mind answering their questions. If it helps the lads understand the story, then ask away."

Sir Darwyn, sitting comfortably in the fire pit, said, "Frailbones, if you don't hurry up with this story there'll be no more leaf for yon pipe."

Frailbones chuckled lightly. "And well be it too, Sir Darwyn. As I was saying, I found out where the elf-lass was being held and made my way there. It was a treacherous journey and a worthy story in itself, but I shall hurry things up for the sake of a second pipe of your fine leaf, Lord of the Chariot."

Sir Darwyn smiled as he drew on his pipe and closed his eyes the more to savour both the smoke and the story.

"There was a small band of Wildlander archers who kept the larders full for the mages. I met them one bright day and convinced them to take me in as one of theirs. They needed someone to manage their wagons and I was certainly the most skilled of their group to do that. It was dangerous for them to hunt this far into the Swords Kingdom. I'd say, where we are now, is mighty close to where I met the Wildlanders hunting game for the mage's table. Aye, over the next few days we hunted closer to their camp which was further south, on the River of Cups.

"Eventually I managed to visit the mages camp to deliver meat. Every now and then I caught a glimpse of the elf-lass, Naroo, and she truly was beautiful. A terrible sadness hung over her which threatened to smother her inner radiance. Not only did the mages' magic suppress her elf-voice but it also suppressed her life-force. Each night they would sit around their fire and take the wee elf-girl out to entertain them. I won't speak of what they did to her but know that it was a vileness beyond imagination.

They were slowly killing her with their cruel spells." Frailbones now stopped to wipe the tears from his face before he could continue.

"I must admit to thee all tonight that the moment I set eyes on the elf-lass I fell in love. She was the most beautiful woman that I had ever seen. But what I witnessed sickened me to my stomach and my heart remains scarred by the pain of her suffering. I swore then that I must save the lass even if it cost me my life.

"It was late summer and the grass was long and dry on the plains. It would only take a spark to set it alight. With the wind behind it, the flames would be driven towards the mage's campsite. I knew I had little enough time already, I could sense the death stare in the lass' eyes and knew she had already begun the journey to the other side..." before he could continue, Clayton broke in.

"Frailbones, what do ye mean? Was the elf-lass trying to die?" he asked.

"Aye, that be the way of it, Clayton. An elf lives forever, as thee knows. They rarely, if ever, have children, knowing that immortality can be a curse in this cruel world. But an elf can choose to end his or her existence if it be so painful to remain living. I knew that Naroo had begun her death song and only I could hear it. I wasn't elf-wise back in those days, I'd never set eyes on an elf before, but I had been initiated in the ways of the inner world and had a way that led me to understand certain things.

"I managed to send Naroo a message despite the mage's weavings. She knew that I was there and meant to rescue her. I could sense both her joy for release but there was also despair as she knew it be a futile gesture. I was in a terrible distressed state meself, so in haste I set fire to the grassy plains. The flames lifted upwards to reach high into the sky and driven by the wind they raced towards the Wildlander camp. The reaction was what I'd hoped for. From my hiding place I ran till my heart was bursting and slid my knife down the back of Naroo's prison tent.

Inside I found one of the mages in a rush to take the elf-lass with him. I stabbed the villainous spider in the back and cut the girl free. As I carried her in my arms I noticed how light she was. It wasn't that she was any smaller than Ziggy here, but her life-force was almost spent. It frightened me and empowered my legs to escape with her.

"I ran as fast and hard as I could with Naroo in my arms. I whispered to her that I would cross the river and take her home. I can still see the light of joy in her eyes as she listened to my babbling, and I still cry at night when I recall the beauty of her smile." The old man stopped and wiped again at his eyes but the tears would not stop. No one spoke, not even Clayton.

When he had finally composed himself, Frailbones continued. "We made it to the river but behind us were the Wildlanders running to escape the fire. The moment they saw me and the bundle in my arms they knew that it was I who had started the fire, and they sought their revenge. I tried to run harder but they were fit and they were angry. I was lucky because there were only one or two archers, the rest were sword and spearmen.

"I was almost to the river, to safety. At each step I could see Naroo... her face was... her face..." He stopped again and wiped at his tears. "She was smiling into my eyes. All through the chase she never stopped smiling for me. An arrow struck me in the back, but I didn't stop. Another creased my head but again I just kept running." The old man absently rubbed at the scar on his temple as he spoke.

"Another arrow struck me in the leg and I fell. I fell but quickly jumped up again, we were almost at the river. I glanced down at Naroo and her face had become so radiant I could barely look at her. But her joyfulness... I could feel it, in my heart. I knew right then that she loved me, she loved me for my stupid, youthful sacrifice." Again he stopped, sobbing quietly into his hands.

The men remained quiet, no-one interrupted. The pipes had all gone out yet no one wanted to break the spell Frailbones' story had woven around them.

"I made it to the river and leapt into its rushing waters. I still had Naroo in my arms, she was lighter than a feather. I could barely feel her weight and then I knew she was dying. The Wildlanders, their mages behind them, threw their spears and arrows rained around me but none hit. Why, I don't know. I have a feeling that since we were in Naroo's elf lands its magic protected us. Or perhaps, in death, Naroo was able to reach across the dimensions to protect me. The river was running fast. Heavy rain in the Hindamar Mountains had lent a liveliness to the river and it carried us downstream for miles. Finally, it left us on a sandy river bank way beyond the eyes of the Wildlanders."

Frailbones stopped talking, he wiped at his eyes and the group silently waited as before.

"There I buried Naroo the Pretty, the elf-lass of legend. Her beauty was beyond anything I have seen since. It wasn't the beauty of face or feature, it was a beauty of spirit. I wasn't drawn to rescue her for her looks, I rescued her because of the spirit she retained to the very moment she died. I buried her, surrounded by her family and friends. Ziggy was there, he remembers. They didn't ask me questions, they respected my grief and my silence.

"I stayed with the Wood Elves to allow my wounds to heal, but by midwinter I had to leave. The memory of Naroo's eyes and her joy for life, her touch upon my heart, was too great and I had to find a way to heal my spirit."

The silence was broken by Ziggy's quiet sobbing. This was the first time he had heard the story. The handsome Wood Elf was now struck with a grief he struggled to contain. It sought to break his heart like it had when he first learned of his sister's death those many years ago.

Frailbones finally looked at his audience and his face was alight with a strange glow.

"And that, my friends, is the 'story never told'." Frailbones looked up at the pale sunrise. "I can feel Naroo's presence now. Each time I draw near to the River of Cups I have a longing and a sadness that hurts. But it also lifts me higher knowing that what I did that day was the right and honourable thing. Truth be told, I wish I had died that day beside her."

Sir Darwyn knew that the moment had come for him to speak.

"Frailbones, thank you, now I understand. Your kindness and generosity has always been a welcome blessing to the many that you have mentored and served." The Charioteer stood and gazed at the silent faces gathered around the campfire. Slowly raising his hands as though communing with the sky gods, Sir Darwyn suddenly roared his battle cry.

Then, with tears in his eyes, he turned to his friend and said, "Frailbones, the price for your story is now paid in full."

At this uttering a bright star appeared above them. It slowly descended to rest within the flames of their fire. Standing before them, within the flames, they saw a young elf-girl. She was smiling and it was clear that she only had eyes for Frailbones. They could see that she indeed was beautiful.

The old man seemed to grow younger as he radiated a light to match that of his love, Naroo the Pretty. His aura grew so bright that those gathered could no longer look at him. Frailbones, the modest Pentacles wagoneer, then stepped into the fire to embraced his love. When the warriors looked again the light had gone, and so had their friend.

"Go with our blessing elf-wise, may we all meet again beyond the shadowlands," whispered Ziggy, tears streamed unchecked down his cheeks.

No one spoke for some minutes, they were overwhelmed with the sadness of what they had heard and witnessed.

Finally Follin spoke. "Sir Darwyn, why did Frailbones have to pay for this story with his life?" he asked through his own tears. The other men waited expectantly for the Charioteer's answer.

"Frailbones was shattered by the loss of the elf-lass, Naroo. He carried the guilt of his failure to save her throughout his life. It was this hidden shame that forced him to keep his story silent, thus it was the 'story never-told'. His sadness and shame were so great that he made a pact using the most sacred of oaths, the only time he would tell his tale would be on the day of his death. He has now fulfilled that oath. You may not have noticed, but that old man was over a hundred years old. There were times that he lived in the depths of depression recalling his failure to save his love." The Charioteer's voice softened. "Frailbones was ready, the River of Cups had called him for the last time. I could feel the presence of Naroo, she was here, waiting to escort him to the elves' shadowlands." Sir Darwyn quietly repacked his pipe and passed his leaf pouch for the men to share once more.

"Don't be sad, where he has gone there be love, only love," said Ziggy. He clearly remembered that time of grief many years ago. To the elven people death was a bitter-sweet occasion. Once they had ended their physical incarnation they could never return. They were quite unlike humans whose cycles never ceased, returning lifetime after lifetime.

With much sadness they said their goodbyes to Frailbones. It was a subdued band that set out to meet with Mondy and the girl's only half a day's walk away.

Under the watchful eyes and guidance of Ziggy, his Wood Elf clan, and Sir Darwyn, the two groups were finally united. Soon after setting out on the Swords Plains together they were spotted by one of the cavalry patrols and escorted to the Swords castle.

Despite the incredible awe and wonder they felt as the castle and mountain came into view, there remained a sadness that hovered like a black cloud over them at the loss of their friend, Frailbones. When they discovered that the Wood Elf, Ziggy, and the Charioteer, Sir Darwyn, were also staying in the castle, Follin and Eve felt a little more enthusiastic about their arrival.

Eve, however, remained inconsolable, so Sir Darwyn sat with her and explained Frailbone's 'story never told'.

"Eve, that old man was elf-wise and the day of his death was the hundredth anniversary of Naroo the Pretty's passing. Frailbones had been granted long-life by the elf-people for his selfless rescue of Naroo from the evil mages. But in some ways it was more burden than blessing. Frailbones had made a sacred pact with the powers blessed upon him by the elf-people to only tell the story once, and that be on the day he died. His wish was granted. He is at peace with his lover, Naroo the Pretty. I think you understand the power of love enough to know that Frailbones is now happy and has found his peace."

That afternoon Follin and Eve stepped onto their stone courtyard to be presented with the breath-taking view of the valley and towering cliffs of the Swords mountain. They sat entranced watching the Windmages practising their craft. They would catch the wind currents and fly upwards in ever-widening circles, to then lazily glide back to their platforms on the castle top.

Follin's Meditation - Ten of Swords

In the picture Follin saw that the sun was setting, or was it rising? The man lay face down, immobilised by the ten swords that pinned him to the ground. Surely this meant sadness, entrapment and grief?

Remembering the lessons he had learned from his meditations with each of the Swords pictures, Follin began the process of examining the evidence placed before him. Piece by piece he went through the image until finally he decided to interview the man himself.

"Kind sir, would you permit me to ask what has happened to you?" Follin asked.

The man, squirming in pain, replied, "I have been through the worst of life experiences. I've lost everything. I took the wrong path on too many occasions making poor decisions that ended in my ruin. I failed to do the right thing and then tried to cheat destiny by doing the wrong thing." He sobbed as he finished, a sob of absolute defeat. "I can not go on any further, I wish to lay here and die."

"Does that mean you have reached the end of your journey of sorrow?" asked Follin, trying to correctly categorise each piece of information as best he could.

"Young man, I've hit rock bottom, I cannot fall any further. I am as low as I possibly can go."

Again Follin examined the information provided by the destitute man and sought for greater clarity.

"This means that the only way for you now is upwards?" Follin suggested.

The man stopped his squirming. "Hmm, maybe. I haven't really considered that possibility. What do I need to do so that I may move upwards? Do you have any suggestions?" asked the man now sitting up and pulling the swords from his back.

Follin smiled. "That, good sir, is what I have been seeking these past few years myself. Here, let me explain what I think you could do." Follin gave a summary of the lessons he had learned on his journey through the Swords Kingdom.

When Follin finished speaking the picture faded to be replaced by the King and Queen of Swords.

"Follin, we have been busy watching and guiding both you and Eve. Your journey through our Kingdom has formed your lessons. It is now time to complete your instruction with this, our own story. It is a parallel to the one you just experienced with the Emperor's pictures. Listen carefully."

The King began. "There was once a tribe that, in escaping hardship and terror, discovered an isolated island in the eastern ocean. It was so far from the mainland that no one had ever visited it before. The island was desolate and dangerous and living there was perilous. The people soon learned that only by dropping their petty squabbles and by cooperating could they hope to survive.

"Whenever a conflict arose the people would gather to discuss the problem and then seek to find peaceful solutions. They learned the art of negotiation and compromise and would always seek a solution that satisfied each party. It remained like this for a thousand years. In time all arguments completely ceased. Not a single conflict arose to disturb the harmony of their island sanctuary.

"The people were a happy and contented people. Though few in number they were thoroughly in love with life. All weapons had disappeared over the centuries, even their fighting skills and strategies faded into the dim past. The people had forgotten how to defend themselves because they never had anyone to defend against.

"One day a trading ship, blown off course, dropped anchor in the island harbour and the crew came ashore for food and water. They were warmly greeted by the islanders. These were the first visitors in all the time they had lived on their island.

"The ship's captain soon learned that the islanders had no weapons, nor did they understand the concept of conflict or of self defence. So he told the island elder that he was going to kill them all.

"The elder invited the captain to sit with him in his home and shared his meal with him. When proper protocol between friends was satisfied the elder asked the captain why he wished to kill his people.

'We want your food and water. We need it to survive our trip home in the rough seas,' replied the captain.

'In that case,' answered the elder, "You can have all you want. We have little to spare but please, take it all. We will gladly go hungry to know that you do not.'

'No, I will still kill you,' said the captain.

"The elder shook his head in bewilderment. 'Why do you wish to kill us if you take all you need of our food and water supplies?'

'It is because we need your land. Without your houses and gardens we will perish,' said the captain.

'In that case,' answered the elder, 'You can have our houses and gardens. We can live in the small caves on the hillside and help you tend your gardens.'

'No, I will still kill you,' said the captain.

"Once more the elder shook his head. 'Why do you wish to kill us if you have our land and gardens?'

'Because my men also want your women folk. We've been at sea for two years and my men are hungry for the comfort of a woman,' replied the captain.

"Again the elder reflected, then he said, 'If you ask our women I am sure that they would be more than happy to oblige your sailor's needs. We have a free and open culture and sex is not something we seek to hoard or take, it is freely given.'

"The captain considered the elder's answer. 'Well,' said the captain after some time, 'We will still kill you all anyway.'

"The elder well knew that this was clearly a game that the captain had played before. He answered, 'But why will you kill us if you wish to take everything from us? What harm are we to you? We can work to provide food and water for you if you are hungry and thirsty; our houses and gardens will help you survive in comfort; and our women are sure to oblige if you need them. All you need do is ask, we are ready to provide for your every need.'

"The captain was noticeably uncomfortable. In the past most conversations of this kind had ended in an argument and the murder of his adversary. This elder had offered no resistance nor reason to fight.

'I'm going to kill you all anyway, because it's what I do,' the captain said finally and stood to leave.

"The elder also stood and approached the captain. 'If that is your final answer then we will fight you. You are pure evil and evil cannot be negotiated with.'

As the captain turned to leave, the elder continued. 'You will now get nothing from us. We will destroy everything we have: our food, our water, homes and gardens, and our women will die rather than give themselves to you. We have nothing to lose, we will stand and fight the evil that you have brought to our peaceful island.'

"The captain laughed. 'Ha! You? Fight us? You have no weapons, you have no soldiers and you don't even know how to fight. We shall slaughter you.'

"With great calm the elder walked the captain to the door of his house and watched him walk away.

"As soon as the captain left to gather his sailors, the elder spoke to his people. The tribe understood that they were confronted with the same evil that they had banished from their own souls for a thousand years.

"The people immediately set about destroying their homes. They burned their food supplies and houses; spoiled their wells of fresh water;

the women threw themselves from the high cliffs; and the men stood with sticks and stones to face the captain's fierce soldiers.

"The battle was short, the islanders were all killed and the captain had won his victory. But at its end the sailors looked about them and saw nothing but devastation. They saw the utter futility of their cruel and senseless act. As if from a dream the sailors awoke and threw the captain from the cliffs. With shame in their hearts they pushed their ship off the beach and left the island never to return.

"Amidst the devastation two babies had survived, well hidden by their parents. Those two babies were raised by the birds, the village dogs and by the spirits of the island long accustomed to the gentle manner of the now deceased human inhabitants. The children thrived and slowly the island was repopulated. That island is Runda Isle, it is also known as the Isle of Secrets, it forms part of your own ancestry, Follin.

"The Air elementals taught the children the art of negotiation and compromise which was the hallmark of their parent's legacy. This formed the foundations of the Swords Kingdom on the mainland today."

The Queen looked at Follin and asked, "Do you know who those two children are?" Follin shook his head. "You are looking at them right now. We were suckled by the elementals of Air and imbued their magic. When the Emperor and Empress brought their people to this planet they sought our advice. We recommended that they found their Tarot Kingdom on the four elements of Earth, Air, Water and Fire."

Follin stared at the King and Queen of Swords. "But... but do the other elementals come from Runda Isle too?"

The King answered in his calm, strong voice. "Runda Isle has long been shunned by humankind. They think it an island of the dead, as it is in many ways since the captain's betrayal of our friendship. The people who live there now do so in peace and harmony. To answer your question, all four elements exist on Runda Isle. Our main teachers were the Air elementals who were instrumental in calming the wild ways of our ancestors."

"Follin, before we retire, we would like to know what you have learned of the Swords change point," requested the Queen.

Follin considered his answer for a brief moment before answering. "Your story demonstrates how a Swords Master operates when negotiating with a psychopath. The elder sought clarity from the pirate captain at each juncture. The elder knew that there was nothing to gain by appealing to the captain's strengths: denial of reality and lack of empathy. It is quite clear that the elder gave the captain ample opportunity to engage the change point and to take what was offered which was a win for both parties."

Follin paused to make his own mind clear before he completed his summary. "The change point was offered to the pirate captain many times but he failed to accept it. If he had accepted the elder's offers there would have been no hardship nor ill will. Instead the captain sought to take, yet give nothing in return. At the final stage of negotiations the elder took command of the change point himself, recognising that the captain was unwilling to compromise his position."

"Yes, well noted, Follin," acknowledged the Queen. "When one is pushed into a corner one should always consider a negotiated way out. However, when confronted with a fixed state of mind, one must grasp the change point oneself to do the best for those you are responsible for. Our elder empowered his people by taking the change point from the captain. When one cannot compromise one must act decisively."

"I can see now what the Two of Swords lady was doing in her contemplations," Follin said confidently. "She had her blind fold on so that she would not be manipulated by her opponent's appearance or his body language; she placed her feelings behind her on the island so that she would be clear of mind and not manipulated by her own emotional needs; and she sat patiently as the captain made his demands. The lady *was ready to act with decisive force the moment she had a clear picture of the situation."*

Epilogue

Londar, the young Brown-caps archer, settled into his new life with the help of his friends. His warm smile and willingness to lend a helping hand ensured that he was always a welcome presence in the castle. The Swords archers, the famed Bowmen, took him as one of their own and continued to teach him the ways of the forests and plains. Londar was also asked to join Arthur's games clan and soon excelled at strategy.

During Follin's time in the Swords Kingdom he made it a practice to loose a hundred arrows with the other archers in the castle training grounds. Not only did Follin's archery improve but so too did Arthur's, much to his pleasure.

Sox grew larger and learned that he could escape into the elemental planes to play with Molly and her friends. Follin often needed to cross into the elemental dimension in order to collect him for his walks.

Follin visited his carpenter friend, Argyll, the journeyman woodcarver and this became a regular routine. The two would sit under the covered porch of the woodcarver's work-shed and share a pot of tea and honeyed cakes. While Eve studied complex trade and treaty negotiations from a master in the castle, Follin learned the art of running a carpenter's shop in a master woodcarvers work shed.

When The Emperor deemed their lessons complete Follin and Eve were asked to prepare for their journey to the Cups Kingdom. The group were delighted to learn that Ziggy and Sir Darwyn would join them on their journey. When Arthur heard this he insisted that he, Natalie and Londar accompany them. It had been planned for them to meet with their new Cups friends at a fishing village called Weathersea.

THE END

This story continues in Book 4:

'The Fool's Journey through the Tarot Cups'

Astrological Correspondences with the Tarot

Air - Gemini, Libra and Aquarius – Tarot Swords

Air signs correspond with the intellect providing us with a logical approach to novel situations, knowledge building, communication and strategic planning. The computer, communications, teaching and education sciences are primarily the realm of the Air signs. It is through their logic that modern science helps us sift through the illusions that abound in our world of internet and social media obfuscation.

Air communicates and negotiates, they use the power of their mind to distribute information. They often show mastery in the use of language and language structure. Many are seen in law, marketing, accounting and finance, academia, social media, politics and management of major corporations.

The Air signs excel in magical and wishful thinking, irrational thinking and denial. We see a proliferation of Air thinking and ideas marketed in our world today. They have an extremely well developed aptitude for manipulation of perception, reality, thoughts and beliefs – both yours and their own. Sometimes they can be boring, delusional, ego-eccentric, self-serving, insensitive, intellectual snobs and bullies, and overly cerebral.

Some keywords: logical, rational, denial, realistic, factual, empirical, communicative, thought, negotiation, eccentric, executive functions, strategic planning, goal-setting, structuring information, magical or fantasy thinking.

Gemini distributes information and ideas, encouraging others to socialise, mix and to share what they know. Sometimes they get overly engaged with social media and suffer insomnia, intrusive and excessive thoughts.

Libra communicates and encourages others to join in and engage with others too. They are strong mediators and negotiators. They tend to compromise their own needs for that of others in relationships and can lose their sense of self.

Aquarius is famous for their original thoughts and ideas. They also have an ability to cut through proper process to get to the core of a problem. They can be eccentric and forgetful as their head becomes so filled with ideas that they struggle to slow their mind, sleep can be problematic. This sign is generally the one most commonly in denial and they make the strongest sceptics of psychic phenomena.

Understanding and processing emotion is the primary challenge of the Air signs. We must ask: when logic rules, where is the heart and spirit to give meaning to life?

Keywords – Swords Meanings

Swords are the intellectuals of the Tarot deck, they delight in the simple logic of the mind. The Swords suit itself is frequently in conflict, just look at those cards, but it is in their own mind where the conflict lies. It is in trying to manage their wayward emotions that can lead to internal conflict.

In terms of the art of negotiation as described in this book, the Swords approach this in a highly structured manner. Firstly, they take time to carefully attend to all verbal and non-verbal communication. Secondly, they set the emotional aspects of the debate to one side before entering their negotiations. Thirdly, it is through careful observation and analysis that they grasp the opposing team's intention and style. Intellectual clarity is the key that allows them to locate and manipulate the change point in their negotiations.

Swords easily cultivate strategy, plan ahead, process information and communicate efficiently. That is why Follin is so focused on attaining clarity in what he sees, hears and feels. This depth of understanding can be the difference between making a wise decision and a poor one. The Swords cards illustrate how this is done.

Ace of Swords - initiating an adventure of the mind; kinetic mental power.

Two of Swords – anticipation; closed emotions; stopping internal dialogue; intellectual change point; seeking clarity through silence; separating logic from feelings; waiting patiently to act decisively.

Three of Swords – sadness; a perception of betrayal; grief and loss.

Four of Swords – contemplation; heal, forgive and recuperate; seeking internal healing to release trauma; to forgive self and to rebuild a gentle spirit.

Five of Swords - conquest; a clever win; arrogance; witnessing dishonour; self-interest.

Six of Swords – change; travel a strategic move; recovery from a tough situation; escape to or escape from.

Seven of Swords - deliberately stealing or taking winnings; entitlement; unearned rewards; wining by stealth; a strategic manoeuvre; ninja activity; acting alone.

Eight of Swords - a negotiation strategy to appear weak when the path ahead is clear; patience; bound; trapped; caught in a bind; deliberately disengaging from the outside world; an intellectual or emotional binding.

Nine Swords - tormented by excessive worry; pressing external issues; unresolved issues of a personal nature; tortured to choose between two pathways when neither seems satisfactory; fearfulness; a positive resolution hidden behind a veil of uncertainty and anxiety.

Ten Swords - hitting rock-bottom; it can't get any worse; giving in to the universe is the only option; the end of an arduous and painful episode; it can only get better now.

Page Swords – youthful; bright minded; intellectual enthusiasm.

Knight Swords - sharp of mind and spirit; curious; strategist; in the process of mastering logic and reason.

Queen Swords - intellectual maturity; insightful and cheerful conversationalist; capacity to clarify logic and emotions at the same time; the master of feminine Air qualities.

King Swords - intellectual maturity; honest' quick thinking; problem solving; able to clarify clear-cut solutions without held back by disturbed feelings or confused rationalisations; the master of the masculine Air qualities.

About the Author

Noel Eastwood is a retired psychologist with over forty years professional experience in education, counselling and psychology. Now a full-time author, Noel shares his lifelong interests in psychotherapy, Taoist meditation, tai chi, astrology and Tarot. A gifted storyteller, his fiction and nonfiction works blend ancient wisdom and contemporary themes.

You can visit his website and subscribe to his newsletters on the many diverse topics above.

www.plutoscave.com

www.ingramcontent.com/pod-product-compliance
Lightning Source LLC
Chambersburg PA
CBHW071926290426
44110CB00013B/1491